THE DEPRESSION DIET BOOK

THERESA CHEUNG is the author of 16 health and popular psychology books, including *The Glycaemic Factor: How to Balance your Blood Sugar* and *How to Boost Your Immune System*. She also co-authored the best-selling *PCOS Diet Book* and has contributed features to *Here's Health, Health Plus, NHS Mother and Baby, You Are What You Eat, Red, She* and *Prima* magazines.

Overcoming Common Problems Series

Selected titles

A full list of titles is available from Sheldon Press,
36 Causton Street, London SW1P 4ST and on our website at
www.sheldonpress.co.uk

Overcoming Common Problems

The Depression Diet Book

Theresa Cheung

sheldon PRESS

First published in Great Britain in 2006

Sheldon Press
36 Causton Street
London SW1P 4ST

British Library Cataloguing-in-Publication Data

A catalogue record for this book is available from the British Library

ISBN-13: 978–0–85969–989–1
ISBN-10: 0–85969–989–7

1 3 5 7 9 10 8 6 4 2

Typeset by Deltatype Limited, Birkenhead, Merseyside
Printed in Great Britain by Ashford Colour Press

Contents

Introduction

When you are depressed, the last thing you may feel like doing is taking care of your diet. While you doubtless know you should concoct a healthy salad for lunch, in practice you may be more likely to grab the nearest thing you can find. You may open the fridge door, and just stare at the fresh red cabbage waiting to be diced up with a handful of sunflower seeds and a rinsing of lemon juice and olive oil. But somehow it is all too much trouble, the fridge door slides shut, and you maybe reach for the last stale doughnut in the bag, or a lump of cheese and some biscuits, or a sweet milky coffee and a chocolate bar. Or you can't face anything you've got in the house, and go out to buy some junk food. Or, you simply don't bother at all – you just couldn't care less about eating.

It is an awesome thought that these apparently minor decisions – what you put in your mouth – can affect your entire outlook on life and yourself. The food you take into your body can make a tremendous difference to the way you feel – even when you don't believe it. The key point is that, when you eat, you are feeding not just your stomach, but your brain. Your brain is obviously key in depression – and indeed it may be screaming out for the right nutrients. Your brain is what manufactures the chemicals implicated in depression. Food can, quite simply, change this. When you feed your brain right, you often start to *feel* right.

This book explains exactly what the brain and body need for optimum mental and physical health. Most mental health experts now recognize that what you eat plays a major role in depression. There is a wealth of evidence linking what we eat to how we feel. For instance, a 'Feeding Minds' report released in January 2006 by the Mental Health Foundation[1] and the UK group Sustain revealed that changes to the human diet in the last 50 years or so could be an important factor behind the major rise of mental illness in the country. According to both organizations, significant changes in the way food is produced and manufactured have not only reduced the amounts of essential fats, vitamins and minerals consumed, but have also disturbed the balance of nutrients in the foods eaten. As a result of both the quantity and quality of the evidence, the report proposed that the changes to the food system seen in the past century may be partly responsible for the increased incidence of depression and behavioural problems in this same time period.

Estimated to affect up to one in five Britons at some point in their lives, depression costs the UK £100 billion a year in medication, benefits and lost working days. Depressive disorders also affect approximately 18.8 million American adults, or about 9.5 per cent of the US population aged 18 and above in a given year.

Instead of causing us to feel helpless, all this research brings good news for the many millions of people whose lives are blighted by depression. What you eat really *can* change your state of mind, and, using the latest scientific research, this book explains how diet can be a powerful tool in preventing and treating symptoms of depression. After a brief overview of depression and its causes, it offers a practical plan for nutritional self-help and shows you how to beat depression and its symptoms.

Although the dietary guidelines given here are designed to ease depression, it is reassuring to note that they also fit the standard requirements for a healthy diet – so following the guidelines will not only help you feel happier, but healthier too. The only drawback to the dietary approach is that although it can give mood an immediate lift, it may take a few weeks or more before lasting positive results can be seen. But, as anyone with depression will agree, it is certainly worth persevering in order to gain relief from the dark misery of this condition.

Of course, if you are *very* depressed, you may need more help than a change of diet, so do not hesitate to contact your GP or other health professional if you think you are suffering from depression. This is very important. Some people *do* need medication. But the great thing about *The Depression Diet Book* is that it can be used in combination with any form of treatment – it won't interfere, it has no side effects (apart from good ones), and it is eminently user-friendly.

Bear in mind also that, when you are depressed, it all looks more difficult – so don't try to change everything all at once. Break it down into bite-sized chunks. If you read nothing else, study Chapter 3 and follow the seven steps suggested there. Just do one step at a time if need be: for example, cut down on coffee and start drinking more water. Or just start eating breakfast if you don't do so already – this alone can revolutionize your life. Anything you do – even the smallest change – will start to make a difference. And, once you have found how well your body and brain respond when you treat them kindly, it will give you the motivation to continue towards a happier and fuller life.

1

Depression: the 'common cold' of mental illness

Depression is not something you can just 'snap out of'. For many, it is an all too familiar way of life. It soaks into the way you eat and sleep, and the way you feel about yourself and the way you think about other people. Caused by an imbalance of brain chemicals, along with other factors, depression affects your whole body, your mood, and your thoughts. Asking people to snap out of depression is like asking them to snap out of their life. They can't.

Depression is not the same as a passing blue mood. It is not a sign of personal weakness, or of insufficient willpower. Depression is an illness.

Like any serious medical condition, depression needs to be treated, and the good news is that it is treatable. Not only can your doctor give you help, you can also help yourself, as you will see in the case histories below.

This chapter also provides information about depression – what causes it, what the symptoms are, what your doctor might offer you, and what you can do to help yourself.

Who gets depression?

One in four women and one in six men suffer from depression at some time in their life, but the real figure may be higher than this as many people with depression don't seek treatment and live lives of quiet desperation. Only about 20 per cent of people are correctly diagnosed, because depression can mask itself as a physical illness such as chronic pain, sleeplessness or fatigue.

What causes it?

Depression results from a combination of physical and psychological factors that cause chemical imbalances in the brain. Physical causes include: certain forms of mental illness and their treatment; inherited traits; chemical changes; drug or alcohol abuse. Psychological causes include: life stress; negative experiences and loss; high levels of anxiety.

So, as you can see, depression has many contributing factors, and not all of them are obvious. Sometimes, too, it is hard to determine how much depression contributes to a poor diet (for example, when you can't be bothered to eat because you are depressed) or vice versa (that is, how much an inadequate diet is *contributing* to the depression). One thing is certain – whatever the contributing factors are, you can help yourself significantly by taking your diet in hand, as the following case histories show:

Miranda

Miranda, 18, became depressed soon after starting at university. Her parents had just divorced and she attributed her feelings to this. She was tired, weepy, and couldn't concentrate – not a good prognosis for her study. Things started to change for the better when her mother came to visit her and discovered that Miranda was living on a diet of coffee, dry toast and cheap takeaways.

Miranda's mother did two things: she bought her daughter a new set of pots and pans and instructed her in the preparation of simple healthy meals such as baked potatoes with tuna or baked beans; and she also had a good talk with her about the divorce and its repercussions.

After this, Miranda made arrangements with friends to shop at a local supermarket on a weekly basis, where fresh food was available, and to share the costs of a taxi home. Her mood and concentration vastly improved, and she started to enjoy university life.

Susan

Now aged 30, Susan had suffered disabling bouts of depression since around the age of eight or nine, when she remembered crying in black hopelessness as she played with her dolls. Her father was a domestic tyrant who, she later came to see, obviously had a personality disorder – though this was never officially diagnosed, and fear was a common experience for her during her childhood.

When she started her periods, Susan also discovered the joys of chocolate and, a little later, alcohol. Her episodes of depression rocketed, as did her dependence on these substances. She started to gain a lot of weight and to suffer heartburn and bowel pains. Her doctor told her in no uncertain terms to stop drinking, and referred her to the dietician at the clinic, who also suggested she cut out sugar. Susan had just met her future husband, Geoff, and was motivated to obey. Within a week she started to feel better, and a month later was depression-free for the first time in her life.

Paul

At the age of 42, Paul was still a fine athlete, but was moody and irritable. He often lost his temper on the tennis court or in the gym, behaviour that threatened his sporting relationships and activities. At home, he would have frequent bouts of extreme depression and exhaustion, when he lay in bed and did nothing for hours on end. These moods frightened both him and his wife, Naomi.

During one of these episodes, Naomi went out to get an Indian takeaway, and Paul's mood improved so dramatically after eating the chicken curry that she concluded he wasn't having enough protein, and decided to pay much more attention to what they ate. She discovered that Paul was a different person on a diet of freshly cooked meat, fish, rice, vegetables and fruit – previously they had both been big consumers of ready-made meals, white-bread sandwiches, fizzy drinks, ice cream and so on.

The change was a relief to both of them, especially as Naomi too had been getting depressed at the increasing tension between them, caused by Paul's moods.

Moira

Moira, 43, took on a new lease of life when she started eating breakfast. Previously her entire day was governed by fatigue and mood swings. She would go into work in a black mood, and by 11 a.m. would be so despondent and exhausted that she didn't see how she could get through the day. After work she would quite often go straight to bed and stay there, flipping through a book – but in reality waiting until she could just go to sleep.

All this had been getting worse over the past couple of years. Previously, she had had more energy and hadn't really had to bother about when she ate. A nutritionally aware friend strongly suggested that she look at her diet, and particularly breakfast, as

Moira tended to snack on crisps, biscuits and chocolate bars all day, starting in the late morning.

Moira started eating a small breakfast first thing every morning – a bowl of oatmeal with a couple of slices of chopped apple and some seeds. She was amazed at the difference this made to her energy and outlook, and she began to look forward to going to work and enjoying the morning.

Sandra
By 37, Sandra no longer felt she possessed any life of her own. She had had three children in quick succession and had given up her much-enjoyed job as a press officer. She comfort-ate continuously, was putting on weight fast, and spent her days in a domestic scramble, never able either to finish the housework or truly enjoy her children, all aged under seven. She felt her life was over and the future was all swallowed up by her family.

Her sister visited her, was horrified at how depressed Sandra obviously was, and told her a few home truths about how she was 'letting herself go'. This doesn't usually work in depression, but it did motivate Sandra – after floods of tears – to consult her GP. He was one of several at a busy practice of some 11,000 people, so she was daunted at the prospect of going; but, to her surprise, he gave her plenty of time and, far from ridiculing her, immediately diagnosed depression. He suggested a course of SSRI antidepressants (see page 11), assuring her they were not addictive, and also mentioned a Mother and Toddler group that met at the practice.

The medication made a huge difference; for the first time since having her first baby, Sandra felt she was back in control. Meeting other mothers helped. She was then in a position to attend to what her sister had called her 'dreadful doughnut diet'.

The symptoms of depression

The symptoms may vary from person to person, and also depend on the severity of the depression. Typically, though, depression causes changes in thinking, feeling, behaviour and physical well-being.

Changes in thinking
You may experience problems with concentration and decision-making. Some people report difficulty with short-term memory, and

---

Risk factors for depression

Depression is thought to be caused by a combination of physical, emotional, biochemical, psychological, genetic and social factors. It is often impossible to track down and identify each contributing element. Some of the risk factors may include:

- A life-changing event, such as the loss of a loved one or the arrival of a new baby.
- Chronic illness.
- Certain medications, including some drugs used to treat high blood pressure.
- Alcohol abuse.
- A history of child abuse.
- Sustained problems at home or at work.
- Physical trauma.
- Having other family members with a prior history of depression.
- Chronic stress and anxiety.

---

are continuously forgetting things. Negative thoughts and thinking are characteristic of depression. Pessimism, poor self-esteem, excessive guilt and self-criticism are all common. Some people have self-destructive thoughts during a more serious depression.

Changes in feelings

You may feel sad for no reason at all. Some people report that they no longer enjoy activities that they once found pleasurable. You might lack motivation, and become more apathetic. You might feel 'slowed down' and tired all the time. Sometimes irritability is a problem, and you may have more difficulty in controlling your temper. In the extreme, depression is characterized by feelings of helplessness and hopelessness.

Changes in behaviour

Changes in behaviour during depression are reflective of the negative emotions being experienced. You might act more apathetically, because that is how you feel. Some people do not feel

---

The tell-tale signs of depression

It is not always easy to spot depression, but here are some give-aways:

- Feeling sad, hopeless and despairing.
- A loss of interest and pleasure in normal activities.
- Loss of appetite or weight.
- Loss of sex drive.
- Sleeping problems, such as an inability to get to sleep or waking very early.
- Feeling physically tired all the time.
- Difficulties in concentrating.
- Feeling guilty and worthless.
- Feeling that life isn't worth living.

If you think that you might be depressed, see your doctor as soon as possible. He or she may refer you to a psychologist, who can assess whether you are depressed, or just under a lot of stress and feeling sad. Remember, depression is treatable. Instead of worrying about whether you *are* depressed, do something about it – even if you don't feel like it right now.

---

comfortable with other people, so social withdrawal is common. You may experience a dramatic change in appetite, either eating more or less. Because of the chronic sadness, excessive crying is common. Some people complain about everything, and 'act out' their anger with temper outbursts. Sexual desire may disappear, resulting in lack of sexual activity. In the extreme, people may neglect their personal appearance, even neglecting basic hygiene. Needless to say, someone who is as depressed as this does not do very much, so work productivity and household responsibilities suffer. Some people even have trouble getting themselves out of bed.

Changes in physical well-being

Chronic fatigue, despite spending more time sleeping, is common. Some people can't sleep, or don't sleep soundly. These individuals lay awake for hours, or wake up many times during the night, and stare at the ceiling. Others sleep for many hours, even most of the day, although they still feel tired. Many people lose their appetite, feel slowed down by depression, and complain of many aches and pains. Others are restless, and can't sit still.

Now imagine these symptoms lasting for weeks or even months. Imagine feeling this way almost all of the time. Depression is present if you experience many of these symptoms for at least several weeks.

Different types of depression

It may help you to realize that depression can come in different shapes and forms. Some of the different types of depression include the following:

Major depression

A person suffering from major depression experiences persistent low moods or sadness, or loss of interest or pleasure in most activities over a period of at least two weeks. Not everyone with major depression experiences the same symptoms, but the more severe the depression, the more symptoms are experienced. Major depression has a severe impact on daily life – interfering with work, school or social activities.

People with major depression may feel despair and hopelessness; their energy levels may be extremely low, and they may find it hard to motivate themselves to do even the simplest of daily tasks. People with major depression also commonly experience low self-esteem and thoughts of death and suicide. It is important to get *immediate* help if you are having suicidal thoughts.

Bipolar disorder

Bipolar disorder used to be called manic depression. A person with bipolar disorder can have moods that swing between extreme highs, where they feel invincible, to paralysing lows where they feel complete despair.

This psychiatric illness can be mild, moderate or severe. During the manic phase, the person is optimistic and buoyed by exaggerated feelings of well-being. Their mind is overactive and they need very little sleep but, while they have plenty of energy, they lack

7

concentration. Work and study may suffer. During the depressive phase, the person feels despairing and may contemplate suicide.

Dysthymic disorder

Dysthymic disorder is a long-term or chronic disorder where low mood is experienced for most of the day, on more days than not, over a period of at least two years. Someone with dysthymia may experience fatigue, sleeping and eating problems, and be plagued by low self-esteem, guilt and negative thinking. Cognitive difficulties include concentration and memory problems.

Cyclothymic disorder

Cyclothymic disorder is when a person has mild and alternating mood swings of elation and depression occurring over a long period of time. Because the mood swings are mild, and the elation is often enjoyable, people with cyclothymic disorder often do not seek medical help.

The periods of elation and depression can last for lengthy periods, such as a few months. Often, a person with cyclothymic disorder has a relative who has bipolar disorder, or they may develop bipolar disorder themselves.

Postnatal depression (PND)

Around one in eight new mothers experiences depression following the birth of a child, and this is known as postnatal depression (PND). Usually, the depression begins during the first year of parenthood, and ranges from mild to severe. Occasionally, it may present as puerperal psychosis (also known as postpartum psychosis or postnatal psychosis), an extremely severe form of PND, in which symptoms may include severe depression, delusions, hallucinations, confusion, mania or unusual behaviour.

It is possible that Sandra, mentioned earlier in the chapter, was suffering from a form of PND, which antidepressants were very successful in treating.

Contributing factors to PND may include:
- The hormonal upheaval of pregnancy, birth and lactation.
- A prolonged or complicated labour.
- Physical exhaustion from broken sleep.
- Lack of support, both emotional and practical.

8

- Loss of independence.
- Financial pressures.
- Altered relationships with partner, family and friends.
- A personal or family history of depression.
- A history of premenstrual dysphoric disorder.
- Perfectionist or anxious personality.

Seasonal affective disorder (SAD)

Depression is more common in the winter months and in the Northern Hemisphere, which suggests to some researchers that brain chemistry is affected by exposure to sunlight. This is often called seasonal affective disorder (SAD). Some studies have shown that light hitting the back of the eye (retina) stimulates the brain to make chemicals that lift a person's mood.

Apart from depression, other characteristics of SAD include eating more and gaining weight, excessive sleeping, and withdrawing from others. Usually, a person with SAD comes out of their 'hibernation' in the spring. Paul, for example, mentioned earlier in this chapter, was always a much easier person in the spring and summer – and on holiday in a warm and sunny climate.

Treatment options for depression

Treatment for depression depends on the type, cause and severity, but, as already stressed, it *is* treatable. Treatments are in fact more effective and sophisticated today than ever before, so do discuss treatment options with your doctor and follow his or her advice, particularly about combining different treatments.

Who can help?

Your doctor

Your GP should be your first port of call if you are suffering symptoms of depression, anxiety or stress. Don't be hesitant about contacting your doctor if you feel you are suffering depression – the earlier you go, the better. Doctors are trained to differentiate between psychological and physical problems, and you should always check out depression not only so that you can get effective treatment, but also to rule out the possibility of an underlying physical cause.

9

Dietitian

If you are anxious about food or nutrition, a dietitian can help with advice on your particular needs, especially, for example, if you think you have an allergy, eating problem, or a medical condition such as thyroid problems, or have recently had a baby.

Allergy consultant

Food allergy or intolerance can sometimes contribute to low moods – Susan, as we saw earlier, reacted very badly to sugar. Unfortunately, allergy consultants are thin on the ground in the NHS, but can easily be accessed privately and can arrange testing for particular allergies and/or intolerances. Allergy charities can advise on reputable consultants (see Useful addresses and websites). NHS and private clinics are listed at www.specialistinfo.com. BUPA can be contacted on tel: 0800 600 500; www.bupa.co.uk.

'Talking' therapists

If your doctor feels you need more help, he or she may refer you for counselling, or psychotherapy may be suggested. Again, you may well find it quicker to go privately if you can afford it.

Make sure that you consult a reputable therapist – look for accreditation such as membership of the British Association for Counselling and Psychotherapy (BACP – tel: 0870 443 5252; www.bacp.co.uk), the UK Council for Psychotherapy (UKCP – tel: 020 7014 9955; www.psychotherapy.org.uk), or the United Kingdom Register of Counsellors (UKRC). Make sure you feel comfortable with your chosen therapist, and don't feel obliged to continue with any therapy where you don't feel at ease.

Cognitive behaviour therapy (CBT)

CBT is an approach that focuses on how to tackle your difficulties, rather than focusing on root causes as in traditional psychiatry. It challenges any negative habits of thought, and works on changing unhelpful thinking or behaviour. The therapy is much more goal-oriented and structured than counselling, and is often recommended for depression, stress and eating disorders.

The British Association of Behavioural and Cognitive Psychotherapies (BABCP – tel: 01254 875277; www.babcp.com) has a register of qualified CBT practitioners.

Hypnotherapy

Hypnosis – and self-hypnosis – is a state of deep relaxation and heightened awareness, one in which the mind becomes more open to positive suggestion. It may be helpful if you suffer anxiety as well as depression, or compulsive eating habits.

The National Register of Hypnotherapists and Psychotherapists (NRHP – tel: 01282 716839; www.nrhp.co.uk) and the National Council for Hypnotherapy (tel: 01451 810500; www.hypnotherapists. org.uk) can help.

Support groups

Groups such as Depression Alliance and the Eating Disorders Association can provide information and support (see Useful addresses and websites) as well as further contacts.

At-a-glance treatment options

Don't be intimated by this list – the message is that there is plenty of help available. Treatment may include:

- Psychological treatments such as cognitive behavioural therapy (CBT) or interpersonal relationship therapy.
- Antidepressant medications, including tricyclic antidepressant drugs and selective serotonin re-uptake inhibitors (SSRIs).
- Medications for treating bipolar disorder, including mood stabilizing drugs such as lithium carbonate.
- Regular exercise and a healthy, balanced diet.
- Stress management techniques.
- Addressing any contributary problems, such as relationship difficulties.
- Counselling, including psychotherapy.
- In the case of seasonal affective disorder (SAD), bright light therapy (BLT). This may be used to stimulate the brain to make mood-enhancing chemicals.
- Electroconvulsive therapy (ECT). This is used in cases of severe, life-threatening depression that does not respond to other forms of treatment.
- Hospitalization. This option is followed in a case of very severe depression, threatened suicide or a suicide attempt.

Things to remember

- Depression is a complicated illness that involves a number of factors, such as genes, environment, diet, lifestyle, brain chemicals, psychology and personality.
- The different types of depression include major depression, bipolar disorder, dysthymic disorder, cyclothymic disorder, postnatal depression and seasonal affective disorder.
- There are a wide range of treatment options available.
- Eating well is something you can do every day to give yourself a lift.
- *Always* seek help if you feel depressed.

Self-help options

There are things you can do to help yourself if you feel depressed, including exercise, light therapy and stress management, all of which will be discussed later. By far the most powerful self-help tool, however, is to take a look at your diet. As you will see in Chapter 2, what you eat changes the way you feel, but if you are experiencing some or most of the symptoms of depression, it is vital that you seek advice first from your doctor or counsellor to discuss the best form of treatment for you.

Once you have consulted with your doctor, you may find that a change in diet is all you need to boost your mood, or you may decide to take some course of medication, therapy or treatment once you have been diagnosed with depression. Whatever you decide, a good diet is the essential foundation for recovery – and it works in conjunction with all kinds of medications and therapy for depression. In other words, a healthy mood-boosting diet will maximize your chances of recovery whether you are having treatment or not.

Another reason why food is so important is that it is something you can control. Feelings of powerlessness can be overwhelming if you are depressed, but changing your diet can transform these into a more positive outlook because it is something you can take charge of every day. The positive lift you get from feeling that each day you are doing something to boost your mental and physical health is a great feeling to have when you are battling with feelings of worthlessness. Having a daily dose of self-help on a plate can be incredibly energizing and motivating.

2

The food and mood link

Is there a relationship between your diet and depression? Does a poor diet increase your risk of depression or make existing depression worse? Can you improve your mood by improving your diet? The answers to these three questions are . . . yes, yes and yes! Scientific research on the impact of food on mood has confirmed that an inadequate diet can cause, or contribute to, depression. Here's just some of the evidence:

When adolescents do not have enough to eat they are much more likely to experience dysthymia (a type of long-term depression), to have thoughts about death, to want to die, and to have attempted suicide.[2] Miranda's mother (Miranda was described in the previous chapter) was upset by her daughter's fear that her life was over and that something terrible was going to happen. Miranda's fears evaporated once she had adjusted her diet.

Another study[3] involving 724 single, low-income women found that those who did not have sufficient food were more likely to experience major depression.

When individuals who are depressed are put on a diet that causes tryptophan levels to decrease, depression is more common. Tryptophan is an amino acid found in many high-protein foods.[4] Again, we saw in Chapter 1 how Paul's mood went down because his diet did not include enough protein – and went up again after a meal containing chicken.

Dieting[5] is the leading cause of depression in both overweight and non-overweight people. This is because starving reduces levels of serotonin and can trigger depression.

A deficiency in magnesium can cause anxiety, irritability and hypersensitivity to noise. It has also been linked to an increased risk of depression.[6]

One study[7] that measured the level of magnesium and calcium in the cerebrospinal fluid of individuals who are depressed and suicidal found higher levels of calcium in those who were depressed, and lower levels of magnesium in those who were suicidally depressed.

Repeatedly, diet for depression research[8] has found that insufficient consumption of antioxidant vitamins, folate and Vitamin B6 and Vitamin B12 is associated with depression.

We saw in Chapter 1 that Moira ate a dreadful diet – and her mood and energy certainly matched. Low levels of iron not only increase the risk of fatigue and poor concentration, but also depression.[9] Her energy and concentration improved simply by eating breakfast.

Research[10] has indicated that a diet high in simple carbohydrates[11] (sugars) has been linked to an increased risk of depression.

A diet low in essential fatty acids[12] has been linked to an increased risk of depression and behavioural problems.

Although more research[13] is needed, the sweetener aspartame may contribute to depression as well as other psychiatric and non-psychiatric problems.

How does diet contribute to depression?

Basically, your brain is calling out for the right nutrients, and only you can provide them via the food you eat.

Chemicals called neurotransmitters relay nerve impulses throughout your body. These nerve impulses make up the communication system that your brain and nerves use to carry out many functions. The neurotransmitters that seem to have the most impact on your moods are serotonin, dopamine, noradrenaline (also called norepinephrine), glutamine, gamma aminobutyric acid (GABA) and endorphins – often called 'feel good' chemicals.

Your body produces these important neurotransmitters from the nutrients that you consume.[14] Amino acids, vitamins, enzymes, minerals, fatty acids, proteins and complex carbohydrates are all needed. When your diet is insufficient, your body does not have what it needs to produce neurotransmitters. The result can be mood swings, depression and other psychological symptoms.

Not consuming enough of the right nutrients is not the only dietary problem, however. Taking unhealthy substances or toxins into your body by eating a poor diet[15] may also increase your risk of getting depression. The following are all thought to increase the risk: processed foods, foods high in sugar, foods with chemicals, additives and preservatives, alcohol, caffeine and unfiltered tap water. Some of these substances, such as sugar – including honey, fructose, dextrose, maltose, lactose, and sucrose – cause your body to use up

15

vitamins and minerals without adding anything positive or health-giving.

Consuming sugar and simple carbohydrates, such as white bread and pastries, also causes your blood sugar to rise quickly. Your body then releases insulin and glucagon to break down the sugar, controlling its level in your blood. If too much insulin and glucagon are released, your blood sugar level can drop too low, a condition called hypoglycaemia. When your blood sugar levels are low you may feel tired, low and moody. You may also experience food cravings. Several studies[16] have shown hypoglycaemia and blood sugar problems such as insulin resistance to be very common in depressed individuals.

Other substances that may trigger shifts in mood, such as caffeine, nicotine, food colourings and preservatives, can destroy nutrients, over-stimulate the adrenal gland, interfere with the way your body processes nutrients, weaken your immune system, trigger hormonal imbalance and cause other harmful effects that can all contribute to depression.

The other problem with a poor diet is the strain it puts on your liver. The more toxins your liver is exposed to, the more easily its detoxification systems are overloaded; and if your liver is sluggish, excessive amounts of toxins find their way into the bloodstream. This can affect the function of the brain, causing unpleasant and erratic mood changes, a general feeling of depression, 'foggy brain' and an impaired ability to concentrate or remember things.[17]

In summary, many nutrients have been found to have an impact on your mood. A diet that lacks key nutrients may contribute to depression, and the problem of insufficient nutrition is compounded by toxins, pollution, sugar, free radicals and modern agricultural practices.

So what should you do?

As we have seen, your diet may increase your risk of depression or make existing depression worse if you are not consuming sufficient amounts of amino acids, vitamins, enzymes, minerals, fatty acids, proteins and carbohydrates. These nutrients are needed by your body to produce important brain chemicals. Also, certain foods can deplete your body of important nutrients, cause blood sugar levels to fluctuate, and over-stimulate your glands, thus contributing to depression.

To reduce your risk of depression via your diet you must check that your body is getting these much needed nutrients. You need to avoid unhealthy foods as well.

Trying to change your diet to ensure you are getting all the nutrients your body and mind needs can be confusing, but the chapters that follow will explain how you can make these changes simply and easily.

3

The depression diet

So, as we have seen, a basic healthy diet that boosts your intake of nutrients and balances your blood sugar levels can not only keep you healthy, slim and energetic, it can also help you beat depression.

The depression diet has no gimmicks or secrets, but it can make a difference to the way you look and feel. In the previous chapter you saw that although diet alone may not cause depression, there is a definite link between food and mood, and that by changing the way you eat you can ease – or even cure – depression. Food is fuel. It helps your body and your mind to function more smoothly. Scrimp on the quality and quantity of fuel, and your body and your mind pay the price.

So how do you eat to beat depression? The principles are basically the same as any healthy diet – sufficient complex carbohydrates, moderate amounts of protein, sufficient essential fats, a minimum of saturated fats, and plenty of water. But exactly why this can help, and how you can achieve it, comes in the simple seven-step basic plan below. To give yourself the best chances of success, make sure that you gradually adjust your diet over a period of several weeks and ease yourself into a new eating routine.

Seven steps to a healthier and happier you

1 *Drink more water*

Drink plenty of water each day. Try to drink at least $1\frac{1}{2}$ litres ($2\frac{3}{4}$ pints – or six to eight glasses) of fresh water each day.

Why?

We can exist without food for almost five weeks, but without water we can't last more than five days. Water gives us life and keeps us alive, yet we hardly give it a thought. Water is an essential, but often forgotten, nutrient. It is also absolutely crucial for boosting your mood and keeping depression at bay.

Your body is made up of two-thirds water, so the intake and distribution is vital for hormonal function and blood sugar balance.

Water also helps to lubricate dehydrated and parched tissues, as well as aiding the body to eliminate waste by making fibre in your food swell and perform its function. It keeps your skin glowing and your cells working, and it delivers vitamins, minerals and other nutrients to your brain and organs. For your liver to break down and excrete toxins and for your glands to secrete the correct balance of hormones, you also need to drink plenty of pure water. If you don't drink enough you will start to feel dizzy and tired and you could get headaches, mood swings and stomach upsets.

How?

It is very important that you drink pure, clean (filtered, if necessary) water throughout the day, even if you do not feel thirsty. If you are feeling thirsty, you are already becoming dehydrated.

Make plenty of your liquid intake pure water, and limit tea, coffee and alcohol consumption. This is because coffee, tea and alcohol can raise blood sugar levels and deplete your body of essential nutrients. Water, preferably filtered, is the best drink for quenching thirst and hydrating your body to help prevent headaches, fatigue, dry skin, sore eyes and wrinkles.

Fruit juices or diluted juices are suitable. However, watch out for fruit juice drinks that seem like fresh fruit juice, but are in fact expensive fakes. Try some of the better-quality squashes and cordials.

Fruits and vegetables count towards your fluids because they consist of around 90 per cent water. They supply it in a form that is very easy for your body to use, at the same time as providing the body with a high percentage of vitamins and minerals.

One way to make sure you drink enough fluids is to fill a pitcher or a bottle with your targeted amount of water and drink it throughout the day. Take it with you in the car or to work, or keep it nearby when you are reading or doing other activities. If the container is empty by bedtime, you have achieved your goal.

Lesley

Lesley really hated drinking water despite the fact that she had been advised to do this quite a few times, by her doctor and friends. When she was out, she made a point of having a few sips every half-hour, rather than great swigs of water, which made her feel slightly nauseous. When she was at home, she would make very diluted squash with lots of ice and sip this through a straw; or she would freeze the mixture as ice cubes and suck on one from time to time.

2 *Eat five portions of fruit and vegetables each day*

Aim to eat at least five portions of fruit and vegetables a day, aiming to have more vegetables than fruit. A vegetable serving is 100 g of raw vegetable and 90 g cooked. A fruit serving is one medium-sized apple, banana or orange.

Why?

Fruits and vegetables are rich in vitamins, minerals and other brain-saving nutrients. Their high dietary fibre content helps to control blood glucose levels and their antioxidants can help boost your energy levels. More than any other foods, they contain essential vitamins such as A, B, C, E and folic acid, and minerals such as potassium, calcium, zinc and manganese, which are all vital for good mental and physical health.

How?

Increasing your intake of fruits and vegetables does not require a major diet overhaul – just tweaking your usual eating habits a little can make a really big difference. At breakfast, for example, try to incorporate produce into whatever you are already eating. Add fresh or dried fruit to cereal or yogurt, warm up some frozen berries and serve over pancakes or waffles, scramble an egg with a large handful of pepper strips and onions, or spread toast with a thin layer of peanut butter and top with banana slices. And if you order breakfast out, just include a carton of fresh orange or tomato juice with your order.

At lunch, add lettuce (dark leaves, if you have a choice) and tomatoes to sandwiches and garnish your plate with a few grapes, a melon wedge, or some cherry tomatoes. Another option: fill pitta bread with deli meat or tuna and a half-cup or more of chopped vegetables such as tomato, pepper, onion, or spinach tossed with salad dressing. In cold weather, try ordering up a vegetable-based soup like minestrone or split pea. Many fast food restaurants now sell side-salads, which can add a 'produce' boost to burgers and fries.

What is 'a serving'?

It is recommended that you have five servings of vegetables and fruit per day.

A vegetable serving is:

100 g ($3\frac{1}{2}$ oz) chopped raw, non-leafy vegetables
100 g ($3\frac{1}{2}$ oz) of leafy, raw vegetables
100 g ($3\frac{1}{2}$ oz) cooked vegetables
100 g ($3\frac{1}{2}$ oz) cooked beans, peas, or lentils
1 small baked potato
168 ml (6 fl oz) vegetable juice

A fruit serving is:

1 medium raw fruit
$\frac{1}{2}$ grapefruit, mango or papaya
168 ml (6 fl oz) juice
50 g ($1\frac{3}{4}$ oz) berries or cut-up fruit
60 g (2 oz) canned, frozen or cooked fruit
40 g ($1\frac{1}{2}$ oz) dried fruit

At dinner, experiment with dishes such as stews, stir-fries, curries, or pasta dishes that mix vegetables with meat, legumes and poultry. Gradually increase the ratio of vegetables to other items. Because the flavours change dramatically, cooking vegetables in novel ways may also pique your palate. For example, try roasting some root vegetables, or steaming fresh greens until they are just cooked, and then sauté them in a little olive oil and fresh garlic. Try to routinely begin dinner with a tossed salad, a fruit cup, or a cup of vegetable-based soup.

Desserts such as warm baked apples with a dollop of low-fat vanilla ice cream, fresh kiwi or strawberries dipped in chocolate sauce, ripe pear wedges drizzled with caramel, or a split banana topped with a small scoop of sorbet or ice cream, crushed pineapple and syrup all contribute to the five-a-day cause.

Moira again

Moira found that she couldn't eat big portions of fruit or vegetables – they gave her heartburn, wind and a 'runny tummy'. She compensated by eating smaller portions more often – two slices of finely chopped apple with oatmeal for breakfast, a small handful of frozen raspberries with yoghurt for dessert, a small mid-morning snack of grated cabbage salad with caraway seeds.

3 *Eat a wholefood diet*

Eat as many fresh and delicious wholefoods as you can. Wholefoods are foods found in their most natural form, like fresh fruits, vegetables, whole grains, legumes, nuts and seeds. They are not processed or refined and have had no nutrients taken away and no colourings, flavourings or preservatives added.

Why?

Wholefoods can help boost mood because your body digests and absorbs them slowly; thus providing your body and your brain with a steady supply of blood sugar over many hours. Your brain needs a constant supply of sugar, but it needs that sugar to be supplied steadily and whole grains do that perfectly. As you will see in the next chapter, if your blood sugar levels are too high from eating sugary, refined foods or too low from skipping meals, this can make you feel irritable, tired and depressed.

As well as helping to keep your blood sugar and your mood balanced, wholefoods are also rich in nutrients that can give you a serotonin boost and a fibre fix. Serotonin is a 'feel good' brain chemical. Fibre is important for your mood because it slows the conversion of carbohydrates into blood sugar and helps to maintain blood sugar balance. It ensures digestion is healthy, fat absorption is controlled, toxins are removed from the body, and energy is released.

How?

In addition to fruits and vegetables (see above), get the rest of your wholefoods from complex, low to moderate Glycaemic Index (GI) carbohydrates. In the Glycaemic Index, carbohydrate foods are classed by how quickly they are turned into blood sugar by the body. The higher a food appears on the list, the more likely it is for your brain to get a sugar overload. The lower a food's GI rating is, the more slowly the food will be converted into blood sugar and the happier your brain will be.

If the GI tables all sound a bit complicated to you, as a rough guide go for foods that are fresh and unprocessed and avoid ones that are processed and refined. This means eating more fruits and vegetables, more whole grains (choose brown bread, rice and pasta as opposed to white bread, rice, etc.), legumes (beans, peas and lentils) and also nuts and seeds. You also need to avoid over-cooking your food as this destroys nutrients and increases the sugar content.

Taking into account your fruit and veggies, you should aim for about four portions of whole grains a day. One serving is one slice of bread, or half a cup of cereal, rice or pasta. Wholefood carbohydrates should make up about 50 per cent of your diet.

There are several easy ways you can increase your intake of wholefoods:

- Try wholegrain bread and cereals with some vegetable dips, fruit toppings or low-fat cottage cheese.
- Try a different grain each week. Use oats, rye, barley, millet, brown rice, corn or buckwheat. Millet and quinoa also taste great and are simple to cook. If you are intolerant of grains, in particular wheat, steer clear of them and make an appointment with your doctor, a dietician or nutritionist to discuss healthy alternatives.
- Add a sprinkling of nuts and/or seeds to your meal or cereal. If you have never really included nuts and seeds in your diet before, don't just reach for the peanuts; instead, have fun experimenting with all the different varieties. Sunflower and pumpkin seeds are delicious. Almonds and walnuts are tasty and crunchy.
- Experiment with legumes in your cooking. Lentils, peas and beans come in a number of different varieties and are extremely versatile – not to mention hearty and satisfying.

Miranda again

As a student, Miranda valued the cheaper legumes such as yellow peas, which, with ham, made a delicious and satisfying soup. She also loved dahls made from red lentils. Porridge made in the microwave was her other great stand-by, made in a minute and varied with a sprinkling of seeds, dried fruit or nuts. Baked apples were also incredibly easy to cook, and comforting.

For vegetarians and vegans

If you look at the diet of most vegetarians and vegans, protein intake tends to be low. So if you are a vegetarian, it is vital that you get enough protein. Below are some suggestions to help you do this:

- You need to replace animal protein with other food sources such as low-fat dairy products, pulses, legumes, nuts, seeds, grains and cereal, otherwise deficiencies in Vitamin B12 (almost only found in meat), Vitamin D and iron are likely to trigger nutritional and hormonal imbalance and make your symptoms worse.
- If you are the only vegetarian in your household, make sure you substitute pulses, beans, wholegrain cereals, dairy products, tofu products or Quorn instead of just leaving the meat part out of the meal.
- Choose cereals fortified with vitamins, especially Vitamin B12. And don't forget Marmite – this is a good source of Vitamin B12.
- Try to eat a large portion of dark-green leafy vegetables every day and $\frac{1}{2}$ to $\frac{3}{4}$ of a pint of semi-skimmed milk a day to ensure your calcium intake is adequate. If you are dairy intolerant, you can get your calcium from soya yogurts and milks or nut milks.
- Eat dried fruits, pulses, green vegetables and wholegrains for fibre and iron. Cocoa powder and dark chocolate is a good source of iron too.

4 Eat good-quality protein with every meal

Eat two to five portions of protein each day, including vegetable sources such as beans, lentils and tofu. Also include low-fat dairy products, lean meat (chicken, turkey), eggs, soya milk, nuts and seeds. One portion is about 87 g (3 oz) of cooked meat or fish (about the size of a deck of playing cards), one egg or half a cup of beans.

Why?

Protein helps maintain blood sugar balance and gives your body the steady sugar supply and amino acids it needs to manufacture brain

- Consume at least 30 g (1 oz) of pulses, nuts and seeds every day for protein and EFAs (essential fatty acids).
- Eat at least one serving of low-fat cheese or cottage cheese a day for protein and calcium – or soya or tofu portion.
- Eat a total of three to four eggs a week.
- Choose margarine or butter fortified with Vitamins D and E in a vegetarian spread. You can get Vitamin D from sunlight as well, and Vitamin E from nuts and seeds.

If you are vegan and don't eat any meat or dairy products, the risk of nutritional deficiencies is higher. You need to seek expert advice from a doctor or nutritionist. The Vegan Society website has a great deal of useful information. The biggest concerns about veganism include the need to make sure you get enough protein and Vitamin B12. The American Diabetic Association, however, states that soya protein has been shown to be nutritionally equivalent in protein value to animal protein. Nuts, seeds, grains, pulses and vegetables are other good sources of protein. And although Vitamin B12 is only found in animal foods, vegans cope because requirements for this vitamin are very small. Yeast extracts used as food flavourings are often high in Vitamin B12 and vegans need to ensure they consume such foods regularly or other products, like cereals, with a guaranteed Vitamin B12 content. You can also take a B-complex supplement that includes B12.

cells. Another reason why protein is so essential is that it contains amino acids such as tryptophan. Several amino acid deficiencies are particularly associated with depression and alteration in mood. Tryptophan, in particular, is very important for combating depression as it helps to produce Vitamin B3 and serotonin. You can find it in meat, soya protein, peanuts and brown rice.

How?

Since your body cannot store protein as it does carbohydrate and fat, you need a constant and daily supply of it. You need to make sure that you eat a little protein with every meal and snack because, when combined with carbohydrates, protein helps to slow down the absorption of sugar. Good sources of protein that are low in unhealthy saturated fats include chicken, turkey, oily fish, avocado, low-fat dairy products, eggs, soya beans, split peas, kidney beans, peas, wheatgerm, lima beans, black-eyed peas, lentils, black beans and grains such as quinoa.

Paul again

As we saw in Chapter 1, Paul was suffering from insufficient protein. The problem was that he found eating a lot of meat too 'heavy'. His wife Naomi was a traditional and rather unimaginative cook, but was willing to do anything to help to shift Paul's difficult moods! She learned to slow down while shopping and to take the time to look for alternatives to meat such as fish, eggs, beans and lentils. It just meant a bit more thought rather than any radical change in their diet – the homely baked beans on wholemeal toast, for example, was a perfect way of upping Paul's protein.

5 *Get enough essential fatty acids*

As a guideline, calories from fat should make up around 20–25 per cent of your total calories; protein is the same, and carbohydrates (wholefood ones) around 50 per cent. You should try to obtain as little fat as possible from saturated fats or the trans-fatty acids found in many processed foods, and as much as possible in the form of essential fats.

Why?

To function optimally, your brain cells require very specialized fats – in particular, omega-3 essential fats, found in oily fish, such as sardines and mackerel, as well as in walnuts and green leafy vegetables. It appears that omega-3 essential fats, like DHA found in fish, manipulate brain chemicals to boost mood. On top of all that, high-quality dietary fat slows down the absorption of sugar and is a great blood sugar stabilizer – and stable blood sugar means less depression and greater mental focus.

How?

If you are eating a very low-fat diet, this means your brain isn't getting the essential fats it needs to boost your well-being, so make sure you get enough. Cold water fish such as sardines, salmon or tuna are great sources of DHA and you should aim to eat fish at least twice a week. If you don't eat fish, try DHA-rich seaweeds or boost your fatty acid intake with pumpkin seeds, flax seeds (linseeds) or hemp seeds.

Karen
Aged 35, Karen was always trying to diet and had it firmly fixed in her mind that 'fat was bad'. In addition, she simply didn't eat enough. She would become tearful, over-sensitive and irritable, flaring up at the least little thing. After reading a magazine article about 'good' and 'bad' fats, she allowed herself to relax and experiment. To her delight, she felt better and also lost a small amount of weight.

6 *Spice up your life*
Instead of salt, use herbs, spices, lemon juice or ginger to flavour your food.

Why?
Salt can cause fluid retention, which will make you feel bloated and heavy. It can also raise blood pressure, which increases your risk of kidney and liver problems and heart disease.

How?
Salt is found naturally in many foods. You can't avoid salt altogether, but you can take steps to reduce your sodium (salt) intake:

- Aim for less than 5 g of salt a day and less than 2 g of sodium per day.
- Try to get out of the habit of adding unnecessary salt in cooking. Taste before you add salt and try to wean yourself off it and to experience the tangy flavours of herbs, juices and spices.
- The following foods are very high in salt and should be avoided, if possible: smoked salmon, dried fish, pickled herrings, smoked bacon, salt dried beef, ham and other salt-preserved meats. Instead of salty preserved meat, choose the fresh alternative, like fresh salmon, lean beef, fresh vegetables.

- Instead of salt, experiment with herbs and spices or other alternatives: basil, chervil, chives, dill, fennel and garlic work well with salads. Thyme, tarragon and parsley can really enhance the flavour of meat, fish, vegetables and potatoes. Wine is a wonderful flavour-enhancer. When it is boiled, the alcohol evaporates, leaving behind the aromatic essence of the wine. Mustard really brings out the flavour of cheese. Have fun experimenting with spices, or alternatives to salt, until you find those you like best.

By making simple changes like the ones mentioned above, you will gradually be able to adjust to a less salty diet and learn to appreciate the more subtle flavours that were hidden by the overpowering taste of salt.

Paul again
Paul was an acknowledged salt addict – so was his wife, Naomi. Here, however, she led the way in weaning them both off it as she suffered terrible pre-menstrual bloating and felt that salt made it worse. Without telling him, she gradually reduced the salt levels in their food. Previously they had been eating lots of ready-made meals, too, which also increased their salt intake. Switching to home-cooked food made a big difference.

7 *Get snacking*

Eat little and often. Start the day with a good breakfast, have a mid-morning snack, followed by lunch, a mid-afternoon snack, and then supper.

Why?
Research has shown that people who divide their total daily food intake into mini meals and snacks evenly distributed throughout the day maintain a more even temperament, and are less prone to fatigue, insomnia and depression. This is because eating little and often helps to keep your blood sugar levels stable – and if your blood sugar levels are stable, your brain is happy.

Skipping meals is the worst possible way to diet, because if you skip meals your metabolism slows down. It is also bad news for your brain which, as we have seen, requires a constant and steady supply of glucose to function at its best.

Healthy snack ideas

- A tablespoon of dried fruits: these are low in fat and have a low Glycaemic Index figure, which means they are absorbed slowly from the stomach into the bloodstream and make you feel fuller and happier for longer. Dried fruits are also high in energy-boosting iron and fibre.
- Berry mix: in a large bowl, mix blueberries, raspberries, blackberries and cherries. This is a very healthy fruit snack. It is low in fat and contains a lot of vitamins and minerals to beat depression. You may also want to add some calcium-rich low-fat natural yogurt.
- Fruit smoothies: this is a low-fat energy-boosting snack bursting with nutrients that tastes delicious.
- Two handfuls of raw vegetables: dip carrots, celery, pepper, mushrooms or courgettes in one tablespoon of reduced-fat hummus or salsa. Vegetables are a healthy treat because they are high in antioxidants, which are the naturally occurring compounds that help to protect your body and brain from disease.
- A cup of low-fat hearty vegetable, lentil or pumpkin-flavoured soup: the vegetables provide powerful antioxidant energy-boosting benefits and the soup will fill you up for hours.
- Cold beans: they have little fat, but heaps of key nutrients, including the B vitamin folic acid, copper, zinc, magnesium and potassium. They are also a great source of protein (usually found in higher-fat foods), fibre and the complex carbs that can stabilize blood sugars, keep hunger at bay, and keep you happy.

How?

Kick-start your mind and your metabolism with a good breakfast, and a few hours later enjoy a mid-morning snack, followed by lunch, a teatime snack and then supper. All you need to get right is balancing what you eat at each of these meals. Obviously they do not need to be large meals as this overloads your brain with too much sugar, but you should combine wholefoods with small amounts of high-quality protein and fat.

Breakfast is often the meal that is completely ignored, but it is the most important meal. It gives you energy and sets you up for the day. You may not feel like eating when you wake up in the morning, so try to give yourself a little time before your first meal. You could, for example, prepare some healthy snacks to eat later in the day.

Moira again

Moira was a demon snacker and hated big meals. Once she got the hang of breakfast, however, and saw how much better she felt when she ate it, she followed it up with several healthy snacks a day. An important point for her was that neither breakfast nor her other meals were, or had to be, huge – she definitely preferred small portions.

Making your depression diet a success

The depression relief guidelines in this chapter centre around the following: fresh wholefoods, fruits and vegetables, quality protein and healthy fat to balance your blood sugar levels and boost your mood.

With all the mood-boosting benefits of healthy eating you will be keen to get it right, but try not to set yourself up for failure. Remember the 80/20 rule: you simply can't eat healthily all the time, so aim for 80 per cent of the time, with 20 per cent of time to relax and have the occasional treat. Eating a cake, a pastry or a bag of crisps doesn't mean you have failed; it is the excesses that are dangerous. It is important to enjoy your food and eat healthily *most* of the time, but you can allow yourself the occasional indulgence. No food is off limits in the depression diet.

4

Nutritional healing

In this chapter we will take a look at key vitamins and minerals and specific foods that can help you to beat depression. We will also look at the 'Mind Meal'. The Mind Meal is a practical example of how food can be used to lift mood.

Key vitamins and minerals

In addition to omega-3 and amino acids, certain vitamins and minerals are crucial for healthy brain function and your emotional well-being. If you are eating a healthy diet along the guidelines given in the previous chapter, you should be getting all the vitamins and minerals you need to beat depression. But it is still worth checking out that you are getting enough of the key players in your diet:

Vitamin B

The B-complex vitamins are important for your mental and emotional health. Deficiencies in vitamins B3, B6 and B12 and in folic acid have been found to have a direct relationship to depression. So what is the best way to get these nutrients? Follow the steps below:

1 Eat plenty of leafy green vegetables, cantaloupe, asparagus, beets and brewer's yeast to get enough folic acid.
2 Add enriched wholegrain products, broccoli, asparagus, mushrooms, leafy green vegetables, brussels sprouts and grains such as millet to your diet to ensure you have adequate Vitamin B2, or riboflavin.
3 Spike your diet with soya products, yeast and cereals to get biotin, an important component of the B-complex vitamins. Beef, liver and shellfish are also a good source of biotin.
4 Eat whole grains, brewer's yeast, wheatgerm, oysters and enriched bread for Vitamin B1, also called thiamine.
5 Feast on chicken, salmon, potatoes and wholegrain products for Vitamin B3, or niacin. Peanuts and peanut butter are also good sources of niacin.

31

6 Eat brown rice, soya products, whole grains, bananas, strawberries, leafy green vegetables, wheatgerm and oatmeal to get adequate Vitamin B6, which is called pyridoxine. Other sources of Vitamin B6 include broccoli, asparagus, fish, chicken and watermelon.

7 Vitamin B12 is unique in that it is primarily found in animal foods such as fish, meat, poultry, eggs and low-fat dairy products. If you are a vegan, Vitamin B12 supplements might be helpful.

8 We can get pantothenic acid, another important component of the B-complex vitamins, in a wide variety of plant and low-fat animal sources, including eggs, avocados, mushrooms, chicken and oranges. Make sure you eat your vegetables, especially the green, leafy ones.

Vitamin C

Low levels of Vitamin C are associated with an increased risk of depression. Boost your intake by eating plenty of fruits, peppers, berries, broccoli and spinach.

Calcium

Depletion of calcium affects the central nervous system, and low levels of calcium cause nervousness, apprehension, irritability and numbness. Calcium is present in a wide range of foods. Low-fat dairy products, leafy green vegetables, nuts and seeds (almonds, brazil nuts, sesame seeds), tofu and dried fruit are all good sources of calcium for vegetarians. Most flour is fortified with calcium carbonate, so cereals can also be a good source.

Iron

Depression is often a symptom of chronic iron deficiency. Other symptoms of a deficiency of iron include general weakness, listlessness, exhaustion, lack of appetite and headaches. Good low-fat sources of iron include wholegrain cereals and flours, leafy green vegetables, treacle, pulses such as lentils and kidney beans and dried fruits.

Magnesium

A deficiency of magnesium can result in depressive symptoms, along with confusion, agitation, anxiety and hallucinations, as well as a variety of physical problems. Most diets do not include enough magnesium, and stress also contributes to magnesium depletion.

Most dietary magnesium comes from vegetables, particularly dark-green leafy vegetables. Other foods that are good sources of magnesium are soya products, such as soya flour and tofu; legumes and seeds; nuts (such as almonds and cashews); whole grains (such as brown rice and millet); and fruits or vegetables (such as bananas, dried apricots and avocados).

Manganese

This metal is needed for proper use of the B-complex vitamins and Vitamin C. Since it also plays a role in amino-acid formation, a deficiency may contribute to depression that stems from low levels of the neurotransmitters serotonin and norepinephrine. Manganese also helps to stabilize blood sugar and prevent blood sugar swings. Good sources of manganese include nuts, whole grains, dried fruits, fresh pineapple, green leafy vegetables, oats and rice.

Potassium

Depletion of potassium is associated with depression, tearfulness, weakness and fatigue. Good sources of potassium include: fish, such as salmon, flounder, cod and sardines; chicken; peas; lima beans; green leafy vegetables; citrus fruits; bananas; apricots.

Zinc

A deficiency in zinc results in apathy, lack of appetite and lethargy. When zinc is low, copper levels in the body can increase to toxic levels, resulting in paranoia and fearfulness. Good sources of zinc include high-protein foods such as chicken, fish, low-fat dairy, peanuts and legumes.

The 'Mind Meal'

The 'Mind Meal' is one practical example of how food can be used to lift mood. A survey by the mental health charity Mind found that there is a link between food and physical and mental health. A list of foods that were thought to have either a positive or negative effect on mood was drawn up. Launched by Mind in 2000, the Mind Meal contains foods that seem to make you feel better and think more clearly, and Mind continues to receive positive feedback from people who have tried and tested this menu.

The Mind Meal consists of the following three courses:

1 Wheat-free pasta with pesto and oil-rich fish.
2 Avocado salad and seeds.
3 Fruit and oatcakes dessert.

What the Mind Meal doesn't include is just as important as what it does contain. You won't find artificial additives or added sugars or stimulants like coffee, which, as you will see in the next chapter, can trigger depression. You will also avoid foods, like wheat and milk, that can trigger food allergies.

What the meal *does* provide are foods containing valuable vitamins and essential fats important for emotional and mental health. The oil-rich fish, as well as providing vital omega-3 essential fatty acids, is also a source of tryptophan – the essential 'good mood' protein that is also found in avocado, seeds, dried apricots and walnuts. Absorption of the tryptophan is assisted by the carbohydrates contained in the dessert. The tryptophan is converted into the mood-enhancing brain chemical called serotonin, and the banana and avocado also provide some ready-made serotonin. Because the meal is rich in wholefoods and low to moderate GI foods, it will provide a slow release of energy to keep you feeling good for longer.

The recipe below serves two hungry people, or up to four not-so-hungry people. Preparation time should not be more than 30 minutes, and all the ingredients are available at your local supermarket or health food store.

Wheat-free pasta with pesto and oil-rich fish

Ingredients
250 g (9 oz) packet of wheat-free pasta such as corn and vegetable pasta shells
100 g ($3\frac{1}{2}$ oz) pesto sauce
170 g (6 oz) tin of salmon or other oil-rich fish such as mackerel, herring, sardines, pilchards in brine, oil or spring water, or fresh tuna (canning reduces tuna's omega-3 content).

1 Cook the pasta in boiling water following the instructions on the packet.
2 When the pasta is ready, drain and transfer it to a warmed serving dish. Add approximately 1 tbsp pesto sauce per person and gently mix in with the pasta.
3 Open the tin of fish, drain off the liquid, remove or crush any large bones, and flake with a fork. Add to the serving dish containing pasta and pesto and mix gently together.

Avocado salad and seeds

Ingredients
250 g (9 oz) bag of mixed lettuce or 80 g ($2\frac{3}{4}$ oz) bag of watercress
1 avocado
A handful (25 g (1 oz)) of sunflower seeds
A handful of pumpkin seeds

1 Place the mixed salad in a serving dish.
2 Remove the skin and stone from the avocado. Cut it into small pieces and add to the mixed salad.
3 Sprinkle on the seeds.
4 Serve plain, or with olive oil or the salad dressing of your choice.

Fruit and oatcakes dessert

Ingredients
2 bananas
2 apples
8 dried apricots
8 to 12 oatcakes
58 g (2 oz) (broken) walnuts

1 Peel the bananas and rinse the apples and dried apricots.
2 Cut the fruit into small pieces, removing the apple cores, and place together in a small saucepan.
3 Add a minimum of 3 tbsp of water and simmer gently for 10 minutes or until the fruit is soft, adding more water to prevent the mixture becoming too dry and sticking to the pan.
4 Arrange the oatcakes in the bottom of the individual bowls (you may have to break them to make them fit).
5 When the fruit is soft, pour into individual bowls to cover the

oatcakes. If the fruit mixture contains enough liquid, the juices will soak into and soften the oatcakes.

6 Serve with a sprinkling of broken walnuts.

The Top 14 depression superfoods

1 *Artichoke*: Artichoke has a bile-moving effect on the liver. When bile lingers in the liver, it irritates the tissue, creating inflammation and decreasing the ability of the liver to carry out its function, so you are more likely to feel tired and depressed.

2 *Avocados*: These are a good source of the B vitamins. These B vitamins, in particular Vitamins B1, B2, B6 and folic acid, have been shown to have profound effects on mood – even in those who are not deficient in B vitamins.

3 *Bananas*: Bananas are packed with Vitamin B6, which helps the body to manufacture serotonin, the 'feel good' chemical produced in your brain that helps you to feel and sleep better.

4 *Blueberries*: Sweet wild blueberries are bursting with antioxidants and nutrients that can mop up toxins and boost your mood and your energy.

5 *Brown rice*: An excellent source of protein that provides your brain with a steady supply of energy in the form of glucose. One of the best things you can do to improve intake of brain-boosting nutrients is to switch to brown rice. It is filled with vitamins and magnesium, which also seem to be important for emotional health.

6 *Cabbage*: Cruciferous vegetables, especially broccoli, brussels sprouts, cabbage and cauliflower, are rich in substances that help protect your liver, helping to expel toxins and boost mood.

7 *Cranberries*: Studies suggest that cranberries are particularly good for your brain and your mood because they protect your brain cells from the free-radical damage that normally occurs over time, thereby keeping your mental function in peak condition.

8 *Grapefruit*: Great for boosting liver function and easing depression.

9 *Fruit smoothies and veggie juices*: Fruit and vegetable juices are the cleansers, energizers, builders and regenerators of the human system. A combination of either fresh raw fruit or vegetable juices will supply all the enzymes, vitamins and minerals to aid

your body's natural detoxification, increase vitality, and boost your emotional and mental well-being.

10 *Lentils*: These are an excellent source of mood-boosting B vitamins and folate.

11 *Oily fish*: Bursting with mood-boosting omega-3. If you don't eat fish, try some hemp or flax seeds (linseeds) instead.

12 *Soya beans*: A great source of low-fat vegetable protein. Proteins manufacture neurotransmitters and are important for healthy brain function and help to provide a high level of concentration, calmness and sense of well-being.

13 *Sunflower seeds/brazil nuts*: Good source of selenium, which has been shown to significantly improve mood.

14 *Watermelon*: Red-pigmented, lycopene-rich food – such as tomatoes, papaya and watermelon – improve liver health, and a healthy liver is essential for detoxification and physical, emotional and mental health and well-being.

5

Discover your triggers

We are all individuals, and will react in different ways to different foods. You don't have to have a full-blown food allergy in order for certain foods (or drinks) to trigger off adverse mental reactions, though some people do suffer food allergies or intolerances that can make depression worse. As you will see in this chapter, many everyday foods can contribute to low mood.

There are clear links between anxiety and our increasing reliance on ready meals and processed food, which are heavy in pesticides, additives and harmful fats. Studies[18] show that eating a diet without fresh fruit and vegetables, fish, pulses or nuts deprives the brain of the essential nutrients we need to feel healthy and happy.

In this chapter we will discuss the most common dietary triggers for depression and also take a look at the destructive impact on mood and well-being of man-made chemicals.

Dietary triggers

If eaten in excess, sugar, processed and refined foods, alcohol, caffeine, saturated fat and nicotine can all make you unfit, unhealthy and unhappy. We saw this in the case of Susan in Chapter 1; she was never tested for allergy, but she certainly reacted badly to sugar. To some extent, this is true of us all – but may depend on how much sugar we consume.

Sugar and refined foods

Excessive sugar consumption has been linked to an increased risk of depression. As we have seen, sugar and refined foods, such as cakes, pastries and chips, are easily and quickly absorbed into your bloodstream and this rise in blood sugar is immediately followed by a sharp drop in sugar levels, which makes you feel irritable and low. The key is to keep your blood sugar levels stable and to avoid rapid fluctuations, so you need to lay off the sugar.

But before you start to panic about giving up anything sweet, don't forget that your body can get all the sugar and energy it needs from natural sources like fruits and unrefined carbohydrates, such as grains and lentils. And with the 80/20 rule, you can treat yourself to something sweet from time to time, too – a bar of dark chocolate, a fruit yoghurt, a piece of fruit tart or a wholewheat blueberry muffin are all great choices, but the occasional blow-out won't kill you as long as you get back on track the next day.

So, this doesn't mean you can never eat anything sweet again – it just means you need to cut down. Here are some suggestions to help you cut back on the white stuff:

Cutting down on sugar

Cut out as much processed food as you can (easier now that you are eating more wholefoods in your diet). The US Department of Agriculture estimates that the average American consumes at least 30 kg (64 lbs) of sugar a year, and the UK is not far behind. Most of the sugar does not come from the sugar bowl on the table, but is hidden in our food – not just in cakes, sweets and pastries, but in juices and refined, processed, pre-packaged foods. So get into the habit of reading food labels to avoid those hidden sugars. Check the labels of your favourite sauces, spreads, cereals, biscuits, cakes and bread for hidden sugars. You may think of sugar just in terms of white and brown, but it comes in many forms: cane sugar, muscovado sugar, honey, treacle, syrup, molasses, dextrose, glucose, fructose, maltose, corn syrup, concentrated fruit juice, glucose, sucrose, lactose, honey and other industrial sugars added to processed food. They are all sugars and it is best to avoid them.

Choose brown, not white

Choosing brown rice, brown pasta, brown bread over the white versions means that you are choosing foods made from whole grains – and they include fibre to help slow down your body's conversion of the carbohydrates into blood sugar. This means you get a steady release of sugar into your bloodstream and you will avoid the highs and lows that can lead to mood swings and cravings for sugary foods and that just make the problems like insulin resistance and weight gain worse.

Limit your intake

Limit your intake of sweets, biscuits, cakes, pies, doughnuts, pastries and other sweet baked foods or processed refined foods with added sugar. Eat fresh fruit instead, or choose muffins, dried fruit or wholemeal scones. Look for breakfast cereals that contain no more than 5 grams of sugar per serving. The best bets are wholegrain cereals like muesli, granola, wheat flakes or hot cereal.

Sugar-loaded drinks

Fruit drinks, beverages and cocktails are essentially sugar-loaded non-carbonated soda pop. Most popular brands contain only 5 to 10 per cent of actual juice. If you do choose them, go for high-juice brands, water them down with spring water, or choose freshly pressed juice and add water to it.

Sugar substitutes

Sugar substitutes are not a good idea as they have been linked with problems like headaches and stomach upsets. Honey and syrup sound healthier, but unfortunately they aren't. A tiny pinch of sugar is OK if you really need some sweetness, but it is better to add natural sweeteners like fruit juice or fresh fruit, or try the herbal alternative, stevia, available at health food stores, which is sweet tasting but with no calories.

Alcohol

Many people think of alcohol as something that makes them feel 'good', so it is not surprising that, when depressed, many turn to alcohol in an attempt to feel better. Unfortunately, this is one of the worse things you can do. Alcohol is actually a depressant. Too much alcohol can interfere with the liver's normal functioning (the liver is the organ that metabolizes alcohol), trigger blood sugar imbalances (alcoholic drinks contain a lot of sugar), and cause deficiencies in the very vitamins needed for good mental health.

The risks of alcohol are directly related to the amount you drink, and the time period over which you drink. High-risk use would be having more than five drinks daily, moderate risk would be three to four drinks daily, and low risk would be one to two drinks daily. If you suffer from depression or are prone to depression, it is advised that you avoid alcohol altogether. When cutting down, follow the healthy eating guidelines, eat little and often, and drink lots of water to help clear your liver and cleanse your body of toxins. Once you start to feel healthier and happier, there is no reason why you should not enjoy the odd drink in moderation, say one glass of red wine, beer or spirits a day.

Caffeine

Coffee, tea and chocolate all contain caffeine, and many people with depression rely on caffeine to help to increase their energy levels. Busy mother Sandra was a case in point – she almost lived on coffee, along with white bread rolls and doughnuts.

But, as with alcohol, this dietary measure can backfire. Caffeine can trigger problems with blood sugar, deplete your body of essential nutrients, and stimulate the nervous system, which stops you getting a good night's rest. Over-stimulation of the nervous system also has the potential to raise anxiety levels, and anxiety and depression often go hand-in-hand. So does this mean you have to give up tea, coffee and chocolate altogether?

No, you just need to cut down on the amount you are drinking to one or two cups a day, as a moderate amount of caffeine does not significantly affect mood. There are a number of herbal teas to use in place of coffee and tea that can be both stimulating and refreshing. The roasted herbal roots, including barley, chicory and dandelion, are most popular. Grain coffee, which is caffeine-free, such as Rombouts and Wilson's Heritage, are also favoured among coffee drinkers, while ginseng root teas are preferred by some. Herbal teas made from lemon grass, peppermint, ginger root, red clover and comfrey, rosehip, apple, hibiscus, clover flower and nettle tea can be comforting and nourishing without the depleting side effects of caffeine. Chamomile tea is good for inducing calm and sleep, and peppermint is good for indigestion.

When it comes to chocolate, you could try carob as an alternative, but if you'd prefer the real stuff, eat small chunks of high-quality dark chocolate as it is lower in saturated fat and additives.

It is best to withdraw gradually from caffeine in coffee to avoid headaches. Lower your caffeine intake by drinking grain coffee-blends, diluted, or smaller amounts of regular coffee. Another approach is to first substitute black tea and green tea, which has less caffeine than coffee and can be tapered off more easily. If headaches occur, increased water intake and a healthy balanced diet should ease the withdrawal symptoms.

Bad fats

A diet high in saturated fat and trans-fats is known to trigger obesity and hormone and blood sugar imbalance. Although you need to ensure you get enough essential fatty acids, you should avoid saturated and trans-fats found in meat, full-fat dairy products, pies, chips and biscuits. Here are some suggestions:

- You can cut down on meat and dairy products like cheese and milk by substituting them with fish or vegetable protein (nuts, pulses, grains).
- You can choose non-dairy alternatives such as sardines, spinach and wholegrain flours.
- You can cook with oils such as sunflower or olive rather than butter or lard.
- Full-fat milk products, butter and hard cheese are high in saturated fat, so choose low-fat milk, yogurts and cheeses which contain the same amount of calcium, but are lower in fat and cholesterol, such as skimmed or semi-skimmed milk, cottage cheese and reduced-fat yogurts.
- If you can't or don't like drinking milk, you could try milk substitutes such as rice milks, soya milks, oat milks and nut milks.

Smoking

Cigarette smoking is the biggest cause of preventable disease, and probably the most difficult addiction to deal with. Passive smoking too has significant risks. Just 30 minutes in the company of smokers can damage your heart by reducing its ability to pump blood, according to research published in the *Journal of the American Medical Association* (January 1998). Smoking is also a significant anti-nutrient. It reduces the level of the depression-fighting Vitamin C in the bloodstream. Smokers also have high levels of cadmium, a heavy toxic metal that can stop the utilization of zinc which is needed to lift mood.

The nutritional strategy for smokers is to increase the intake of wholesome foods – fruits, vegetables and whole grains – and to decrease the intake of fats, cured or pickled foods, additives and alcohol. The increased blood and tissue alkalinity that results will help reduce the craving. Adequate fruits, vegetables and whole grains will help to replenish the protective antioxidant nutrients, such as Vitamins A, C and E and selenium, which have been depleted by smoking. Research at St George's Hospital Medical School in London published in the medical journal *Thorax* (January 2000) has also shown that certain foods, like apples, can boost lung health and healing capacity. Organic, unfiltered raw apple cider vinegar is a natural tonic for overall health, especially respiratory health. Take a teaspoon in a glass of water every day. In addition, raw seeds, nuts, legumes, sprouts and other proteins should be consumed. Water is essential to balance out the drying effects of smoking. Since smoking generates an acidic condition in the body, a high-fibre diet helps detoxification by maintaining bowel function.

Allergies and diet

Allergies to certain foods can upset hormones and chemicals in the brain. There have been many published studies linking food allergies with depression, and the most common allergies are to cow's milk protein and gluten-containing wheat products. If you suspect this might be the case for you, talk to your doctor and keep a food diary to see if you can link your low mood to a certain food. If a suspected link is found, your doctor may advise you to exclude gluten-containing grains and/or dairy proteins. Such a diet might in some cases result in a few days of withdrawal symptoms, followed by a substantial improvement in mood.

Detoxing

Although you might associate the word 'detox' with strict weight loss plans, this isn't what is meant here. The use of the word 'detox' in this context means trying to avoid unnecessary man-made chemicals and pollutants that clog up your system, upset your hormone and blood sugar balance, and make it harder for your body and brain to work efficiently. It means you are helping your body and brain to feel better, and not wasting their time getting rid of toxins when they could be repairing themselves and functioning on top form. What's more, many of today's man-made chemicals have been shown to put an enormous strain on your liver and, as we have seen, a healthy functioning liver is an important part of beating depression.

What are toxins?

Every day we are surrounded by potentially hormone-disturbing toxins from the chemicals occurring in everything from plastics to solvents and adhesives, additives, colourings, pesticides and preservatives in foods, chemicals that get into our skin and bodies via our make-up, nail polish, shampoo, moisturizers and deodorants, not forgetting any chemicals such as chlorine and medications passed into the water we drink (a recent report found the antidepressant Prozac, and at least seven other drugs, in the UK water supply), the petrochemicals found in pesticides, plastics, household cleaners – and all the stuff swirling around in the air we breathe, from car exhausts to cigarette smoke.

Our bodies don't need these chemicals and toxins, and have to work very hard to metabolize and get rid of them. In the process of metabolizing toxins, our bodies lose vital nutrients – for example, your body needs Vitamin C to get rid of cigarette smoke – nutrients that we need to feel healthy and happy.

Your 'in-house detoxifying system'

Your body has its own 'in-house detoxifying system' to remove toxins, and the major player here is the liver. Your liver is in effect a chemical-cleaning workaholic that neutralizes and removes toxins and excess hormones such as oestrogen and sends them to the kidney for elimination. Alcohol, fatty foods, highly refined foods, smoking, drugs, xenoestrogens and other environmental toxins can overload your liver, and when levels are too high they clog your liver's pathways. When this occurs, blood sugar levels start to fluctuate, excess hormones can't be cleared, and you are more likely to feel low. With the liver straining to do its job, this will force your other detoxifying organs – your skin, kidneys, lymph system and kidneys – to do double time, which can cause rashes, acne, an excess of testosterone, bloating, yeast infections, depression and poor health in general.

How do you know if you are suffering from toxic overload?

Signs of toxicity are diverse and differ from person to person. If you are prone to acne, you may find that your skin erupts every time you are under the slightest stress. If you are prone to headaches, they may be more frequent and severe. The following are the most common symptoms of excess toxicity:

- Bad breath.
- Sore or coated tongue.
- Fatigue.
- Headaches.

- Weight gain.
- Bowel and digestive problems.
- Allergies.
- High cholesterol.
- Blocked arteries.
- Skin disorders such as acne or rashes.
- Gall bladder problems.
- Foggy brain – your brain is not capable of disarming toxins and is heavily dependent on your liver to do so. This means that if your liver isn't working properly due to toxic overload, it can lead to a wide variety of mental symptoms, including memory loss, drowsiness, inability to focus, low mood, 'woolly-brain syndrome' and a heightened response to alcohol.

How to protect yourself from toxic overload

You don't really need to go on fasts, retreats or adopt harsh regimes, or to take supplements to protect yourself from toxicity. More often than not these harsh measures just slow your metabolism right down. The best way to protect against toxicity is to keep your body's own self-purifying system in good order by giving your liver, kidneys and adrenals nutritional support from a healthy diet, reducing your exposure to toxins, and following the recommendations below:

1 Eat a healthy diet according to the guidelines given previously. Nutrients can help your liver to process, transform or eliminate toxins and excess hormones. A healthy diet can help you prevent, control and repair the damage that toxins have caused, while at the same time working to restore hormonal balance in your body. It is especially important to increase your intake of fibre and cruciferous vegetables. Fibre can help prevent the absorption of toxins into your bloodstream and cruciferous vegetables, such as broccoli, brussels sprouts, cabbage and cauliflower, are high in substances called indole3carbinol, which encourage the elimination of toxins.

2 As far as possible, avoid food and drinks in plastic containers or wrapped in plastic. Don't store any fatty foods (cheese, meat, etc.) in plastic wrap. This is because many chemicals found in plastic tend to be absorbed into food with a high fat content. Remove food from plastic wrapping as soon as possible and don't heat food in plastic, especially in a microwave.

Detox superfoods

Blueberries: Packed with antioxidants and phytochemicals that can reduce toxic damage to liver cells – and blueberries are the detox 'superstars'.

Artichokes: For starters, why not feast on artichokes? Current research shows that cynarin, found in artichoke leaves, stimulates bile secretions, which help to improve fat emulsification and digestion and the expulsion of toxins from your body.

Cabbage: Cruciferous vegetables, especially broccoli, brussels sprouts, cabbage and cauliflower, are rich in liver-friendly phytochemicals that stimulate detoxification enzymes, helping to expel toxins and disarm cancer-causing chemicals.

Watermelon: Red-pigmented, lycopene-rich foods – such as tomatoes, papaya and watermelon – improve liver health, and a healthy liver is of course essential for detoxification.

Wholefoods: As much as possible, eat foods in their whole form – the way that nature made them. Wholefoods also contain more fibre, which helps to remove toxins from your body. Lima beans, soya beans, lentils, nuts and seeds, and whole grains such as barley, buckwheat, oats and quinoa, are high-fibre sources that cleanse your liver naturally.

3 As much as you can, buy organic fruit and vegetables that are naturally grown and have not been chemically treated. There are thousands of types of insecticide, herbicide and fungicide approved for use in the UK and the USA, and some fruits and vegetables are sprayed as many as ten times.

4 Drink pure water. Your body needs lots of water to process waste, but make sure that your fluid intake isn't increasing the toxic burden. It is estimated that as many as 60,000 different chemicals, metals and toxins now contaminate our tap water. Ideally you should purify your home supply of drinking water using a water filter jug, readily available from supermarkets and health food shops, or the more expensive built-in water-filter systems. Alternatively, buy water bottled in glass, not plastic, because plastic compounds are leached from the bottle into the

water. Or drink cooled boiled tap water to get rid of the bacteria and limescale. If you are still drinking tap water and suspect your home has lead pipes, use only the cold for drinking and cooking.

5 Your body sees sugar, salt, food colourings, preservatives and additives as unwanted toxins that increase your risk of hypertension, heart disease, diabetes, depression and cancer. Avoid these substances as much as possible. Processed ready-cooked, canned and refined foods are often high in these (see point 6), so limit the amount you consume.

6 Additives in food have been linked to a variety of health problems, including poor concentration, headaches and allergies. These additives in the form of colourings, preservatives, flavour enhancers, stabilizers and thickeners add to your body's toxic load. Cutting out additives such as food colourings, preservatives and flavourings (usually listed on the packet or can as E numbers) should help to reduce the toxin load that interferes with your hormone levels. The additives that cause the most damage are monosodium glutamate (MSG), artificial colourings, sorbate, sulphates, asparatame, butylated hydroxyanisole and butylated hydroxytoluene. Get into the habit of reading food labels to check what you are actually taking into your body. Watch out for alternative names. For instance, sodium is another name for salt, animal fat is saturated fat, and sugar has many pseudonyms: sucrose, fructose, dextrose or maple syrup to name but a few. As a rule of thumb, if you can't understand a label, can't see any natural ingredients, or the list of chemical ingredients is so long there's barely enough room, leave it on the shelf.

7 Avoid overcooking your food as it can destroy vital nutrients – nutrients that you need to fight toxins. Try grilling instead of frying, lightly steam vegetables instead of boiling them, and avoid all aluminium cookware.

8 Buy natural cleaning products to reduce the number of potentially dangerous chemicals in your house. Or use the tried and tested methods your granny used when there were far fewer chemicals around – such as white vinegar and lemon for stain removal, washing soda instead of commercial soda, or chemical-free liquid soaps and detergents. Use natural toiletries too if you can – make-up, deodorants and creams, etc. Research is still in its early stages, but scientists are investigating the links between the chemicals in deodorants and antiperspirants and breast

cancer. The answer is to buy chemical-free products whenever you can.

9 Go for a walk in a park or a green place at least once a day. Trees give out energizing oxygen. Surround your home and workplace with plants if you live in a city or busy town. NASA research has shown that the following plants can extract fumes, chemicals and smoke from the air: peace lilies, dwarf banana plants, spider plants, weeping fig, geraniums and chrysanthemums.

10 Limit electromagnetic exposure. Commonplace items in your bedroom – from alarm clocks, TVs and videos, to power sockets near your bed – may help to increase the potential of electromagnetic exposure. Purchase battery-operated clocks and radios or unplug electric sockets in the evening. If your work involves VDUs, make sure you take regular breaks – get up and walk around or get some fresh air – every 30 minutes or so.

11 De-stress. If you are having a bad week at work, are not sleeping properly, or have to make major decisions, signs of toxicity can worsen. This is because stress causes your energy reserves to be channelled away from your body's detoxification mechanisms. (The stress management techniques and tips for better sleeping in the next chapter should help here.)

12 And last but by no means least, make sure you exercise regularly. Exercise is a great detoxifier. It boosts circulation, speeds up metabolism, aids digestion, encourages sweating and elimination, clears your mind and makes you feel good. (There is more on the mood-lifting benefits of exercise in the next chapter.)

There is no doubt that levels of pollutants and toxins are rising steeply, but it *is* possible to find health-friendly ways around them so that they don't affect our physical or emotional health. For most of us, healthy eating, regular exercise and avoiding toxins where possible is sufficient to prevent the risk of long-term health problems and depression linked to an overload of environmental toxins.

6

Protecting yourself

To maximize your chances of success on the depression diet you need to combine it with regular exercise, preferably in the fresh air, and regular rest and relaxation, and this chapter explains why.

Paul, whom we met in Chapter 1, was a 'super-athlete', and he really got the most from his exercise once he adjusted his diet.

Moira, in addition to having breakfast, also began to walk to the station some 20 minutes away (previously her husband had driven her there).

Lesley took on an allotment, so she killed two birds with one stone – lots of hearty exercise through digging, and loads of lovely organic vegetables!

If you are prone to depression, the benefits of exercise just cannot be exaggerated. Recent research confirms that regular moderate exercise has an antidepressant effect, and exercise combined with a healthy diet is one of the most natural, effective and healthy ways to combat depression, helping with just about every symptom of it. Study after study has shown that exercise is a helpful way to treat depression because it:

- Increases your sense of mastery. This is very helpful for those who don't feel in control of their lives and moods.
- Helps to balance your hormone and blood sugar levels.
- Keeps your bowels working efficiently to eliminate toxins that your body doesn't need.
- Boosts immunity, lowers the risk of obesity, diabetes and high blood pressure, and speeds up metabolism so that you burn calories faster.
- Increases self-esteem.
- Provides a distraction from your worries.
- Improves your health and body, which can help to lift your mood.
- Helps you get rid of built-up stress and frustration.
- Helps you to sleep better, which can often be a problem when you are depressed.

Exercise also has a direct impact on your mood. When you exercise, brain chemicals called endorphins are released and these boost mood and help you to feel happier and calmer. Studies[19] have shown that it can have a positive effect on both women and men suffering from stress, anxiety, insomnia, fatigue and depression. In short, exercise can make you look and feel better.

It may seem impossible to get moving when you feel depressed, but that is exactly what you have to do. No matter how bad or how tired you feel, getting up and moving around can bring some immediate relief to your symptoms, and getting in a little exercise is an excellent way to work off some of that added stress that you are carrying around.

Keep it simple

The problem with depression is that it makes you feel as if you have no energy. Even getting out of bed can take a monumental effort, so it may be hard to imagine exercising at all when you are depressed. No matter what your thoughts are telling you, though, it really *is* possible to exercise when you are depressed. If you take some simple steps, you can add a little activity to your day to help to lift your mood and work through your depression.

Ideally you should be aiming for around 30 minutes of moderate activity a day. You don't need to do your 30 minutes all at once – it can be spread out during the day and can include such activities as climbing stairs, a brisk walk, house cleaning, walking when talking on your mobile, and so on. All activity counts. You just need to get 30 minutes a day most days of the week. If you don't think you are getting your 30 minutes, find ways to reach this goal – park further away from work so that you have to walk, take the stairs instead of the lift, carry your shopping home, wash your car by hand, mow the lawn. In the long run, these simple changes will help you to feel better about yourself.

Don't think of exercise as a burden. If exercise is just another 'should' in your life that you don't think you are living up to, you will associate it with failure. Rather, look at your exercise schedule the same way as you look at your therapy sessions or antidepressant medication – as one of the tools to help you get better:

• Set simple goals – you don't have to train for a marathon! Set a goal to get dressed and walk around the block. Promise yourself that you will walk around the block at least three times that day. The next day, do more. Try to improve just a little bit each day.

- Go easy on yourself. You might not be able to handle a lot of exercise, so try to feel good about what you *can* do. Now is not the time to stress yourself out.
- Do what you enjoy. If yoga feels good to you, spend a few minutes going through your favourite positions. If you usually enjoy the gym, get your bag packed and hit the treadmill. Even if you are not enjoying it right now, eventually you will. If you used to enjoy dancing, sign up for a class or put your favourite music on at home. If you used to get a kick out of playing sport, sign up for a team or join a club. Don't wait until you *want* to do it – start doing it now. The enthusiasm will come later.
- Make it social. Try to find a friend to walk with you. Talking to people can help to raise your energy and remind you that you are not alone.
- Address your barriers by identifying your individual 'blocks' to exercising. If you feel intimidated by others or are self-conscious, for instance, you may want to exercise in the privacy of your own home. If you stick to goals better when you are with a partner, find a friend to work out with. If you don't have extra money to spend on exercise gear, do something that is virtually cost-free – walk. If you think about what is stopping you from exercising, you can probably find an alternative solution.
- Prepare for setbacks and obstacles. Exercise isn't always easy or fun, and it is tempting to blame yourself for that. People with depression are especially likely to feel shame over perceived failures. Don't fall into that trap. Give yourself credit for every step in the right direction, no matter how small. If you skip exercise one day, that doesn't mean you are a failure and may as well give up altogether. Just try again the next day.

Work with your doctor

Be sure to talk to your doctor about your treatment options and your plans to exercise. This is especially important if you are over 40, have high blood pressure, are overweight, or haven't exercised for years, as you need to check with your doctor for safety guidelines.

He or she may be able to refer you to someone who can help you set up an exercise programme.

How to start moving

You may find it very hard to feel energetic when you are depressed, and indeed exercise is probably the last thing you want to do, but your recovery will be much quicker if you start moving. It will seem like an ordeal at first, but it will not harm you.

If you are reading this sitting in a chair and feel comfortable, why not give the following a try:

- Take one deep breath, lifting your shoulders as you do; open your mouth and, as you do, let the breath out and drop your shoulders. Try to feel like a burst balloon.
- Now breathe normally and lift your shoulders, and then relax them eight times.
- Keeping your arms limp, circle each shoulder eight times in a clockwise position and then try doing this with both arms at the same time.
- Remaining in your chair, raise your arms to the ceiling and stretch as hard as you can before letting them fall loosely down.
- Stretch out your fingers and do eight circles each way with them.
- Gently lift your legs and do eight circles with your ankles.
- If you are not too tired after doing these exercises, stand up and give yourself a shake – like dogs do when they are wet.

Don't stop there. See how many gentle stretching exercises you can incorporate into your day. Stand on your toes and gently lower your heels when you are brushing your teeth, reach up to shelves with both hands, run on the spot when you are waiting for the kettle to boil. Hold on to the back of a chair and do some gentle knee bends. Do some press-ups or sit-ups or gentle stretches while you are watching television.

Building these movements into your daily routine is useful if you don't feel up to walking, yoga, swimming, running, etc. They will all help to boost your circulation, which helps to normalize your brain chemistry and helps your body to expel toxins.

Another way to stimulate your circulation and help the release of toxins is dry skin brushing for about five minutes before a bath or shower. You can buy dry skin brushes from any chemist. Avoid tender or broken skin, moles or pimples.

Get some light into your life

Exercise is beneficial whether you do it indoors or outdoors, but if you do it outdoors, you will be giving yourself a double shot of happiness. Even a little bit of sunshine can help to raise your mood. Try to get outside and exercise in the fresh air. Remind yourself that there is a world out there and you can participate in it as much as you can handle.

It isn't just the exercise, fresh air and the stimulation of new sights and sounds that can help to lift your mood when you are trying to beat depression. It is also worth thinking about something as simple and natural as light.

Have you ever noticed how much happier you feel when it is a bright, sunny day? You feel energized and eager to live it up. In contrast, think about how you feel when the clocks go back and the days get gloomier and shorter and night time falls depressingly early.

Light, or the lack of daylight, may affect your emotional and physical health far more than you realize. SAD, or seasonal affective disorder, is a well-known seasonal depression that affects people during the winter months and lifts during the spring and summer. Symptoms of SAD closely mirror those of depression; people feel low and tired and crave sweet foods. And you may find that in the winter months the lack of light makes your depression worse.

But why is depression connected to light? The answer is to do with your metabolic cycles, which are light dependent. Your sleep cycle is very much governed by the light, or lack of it. When the sun goes down and darkness falls, your brain begins to produce a neurotransmitter called melatonin which makes you feel drowsy and prepares your body for sleep. When you are exposed to bright light, however, your brain starts to convert melatonin to serotonin, which energizes you and makes you feel alert and confident. Melatonin and serotonin are two substances that can be easily converted from one to the other.

You want to have a plentiful supply of serotonin, not just because it makes you feel good, but also because it provides the raw material

Light therapy

To boost your serotonin production you need to expose yourself to either full-spectrum light that you get from the sun or a bright white light. Incandescent lights that you may have in your lamps just aren't the same. If it is summer time or you live in a sunny climate, light therapy is simple. You just need to walk outdoors for about 30 minutes each day – preferably in the morning. Don't wear sunglasses or tinted contacts lenses to ensure that your eyes are exposed to the light rays. Raise your face to the sky (but don't look directly at the sun). Even on a cloudy day, the sun provides the full spectrum of light that the body needs.

To help regulate the production of serotonin and melatonin, it has been suggested that people with SAD and/or depression should also try to eliminate all outside sources of light at night to get their body clock back to a proper dark and light cycle. This helps to orchestrate the correct timing of the secretion of melatonin and serotonin. It might be worth putting black-out curtains up to shut out street lights or perhaps to wear an eye mask to bed.

If you think you need something more to boost the production of serotonin/melatonin, you might want to think about a special light box that can provide fluorescent full-spectrum light or a bright white light that contains no UV

for melatonin so you can fall asleep at night. Without enough serotonin you can end up feeling depressed and irritable with food cravings, and you can also have problems sleeping.

Clearly, too little serotonin and melatonin can play a big part in triggering symptoms of depression or making them worse, and there is something that can significantly decrease your levels of these neurotransmitters – lack of light.

The depression–light connection

Too little serotonin and melatonin and too little light are related. Here's a checklist of the symptoms caused by both:

- Change of appetite.
- Irritability.

wavelengths (UV can cause skin cancer). There are also new systems that use cool-white and bi-axial lamps. The light is measured in units called lux and a typical light box provides 10,000 lux. Daylight is around 5,000 lux and it takes around 2,500 lux to have a therapeutic effect on your internal clock.

Light therapy has also been used successfully to treat the depression associated with PMS, chronic anxiety and panic attacks, severe jet lag, and eating disorders such as anorexia nervosa and bulimia. You can do light therapy yourself as long as you follow the instructions with your box to the letter and don't overdo it – but it is always best to check with your doctor first for advice. The downside of light therapy is that sometimes it can be quite time-consuming; those with SAD may need to sit in front of a lamp for a few hours in both the morning and the evening in the winter months. That is not easy to do, and some experts have suggested that those with SAD should replace their ordinary light bulbs with full-spectrum versions so that they can get a good blast of light during the day. You may also need to give this therapy time to work – a few days to a couple of weeks. If after this you see no improvement, try using your light for slightly longer.

- Tendency to oversleep.
- Low self-esteem.
- Weight gain.
- Difficulty in concentrating.
- Fatigue or low energy levels.
- Reluctance to socialize.

Sounds a lot like depression, doesn't it? So if you have depression, one of the simplest and most effective natural therapies is to get some light into your life. By getting plenty of natural daylight and fresh air you will increase your serotonin and melatonin levels, and boost your mood and energy levels.

Stress management

If you find that your mood gets worse when you are under stress, or that stress triggers an episode of depression, you are not alone. There is a definite link between stress and depression, and stress management is crucial if you want to maximize the benefits of your depression diet. The stress–depression link is explained below.

When you are under stress, your adrenal glands pump out the stress hormones adrenaline and cortisol, which have a powerful effect on your body. Your heart rate speeds up, arteries tighten to raise blood pressure, digestion slows down because it isn't immediately necessary, and your liver releases emergency stores of glucose to give you the energy to fight or escape.

All this means you are primed and ready to fight, but the trouble is that most modern-day stresses, such as missing a train or getting stuck in traffic, can't be resolved by action. You just sit there and get stressed out! Then, if the stress becomes long term, your adrenal glands get overworked and start producing too much adrenaline and cortisol, which in turn can upset your blood sugar balance and trigger weight gain and depression.

Last but by no means least, prolonged stress also affects your digestion, so it means you are not getting the nutrients you need from the food you eat – the nutrients you need to fight depression.

Stress management is essential if you are prone to depression – not just to keep depression at bay, but also to optimize the nutritional value of the foods you eat. The following stress management tips can help:

- Learn to recognize when you are stressed. Many of us have got so used to living with stress that we don't realize we are stressed. Common signs of stress include irritability, lack of concentration, mood swings, fatigue and digestive problems.
- Deal with short-term stress, such as sitting in a traffic jam, with simple relaxation techniques such as tensing your muscles and relaxing them, or do deep breathing to a count of ten. Other techniques for short-term stress include stretching, talking with friends, drinking calming herbal teas like chamomile or lemon balm, having a good laugh, stroking your pet, daydreaming about relaxing places you've been to, or hugging someone you love.
  Research has shown that massage can help to lower blood pressure, improve breathing, boost mood and well-being and aid

circulation. Some experts believe that massage helps the brain to produce endorphins, the chemicals that act as natural painkillers. The sense of well-being you get from a massage can lower the amount of stress hormones circulating in your body.

- Yoga is a great stress reducer, and many studies suggest that it can help to prevent depression. MIND, the UK's leading mental health charity, recommends yoga as the single most effective stress buster. Meditation is another good way to deal with mental and physical stress.

- Don't waste energy trying to change those things you cannot change. Try to identify those situations that trigger stress and, if you can't avoid them, find ways to accept and manage them with the minimum amount of stress.

- Simply talking to friends, family and partners can ease stress. Remember, stress can make your symptoms worse and increase your risk of disease, so create a network of support. It could be your partner or family and friends, but if you don't feel you have anyone you can talk to, a trained counsellor can help you to get in touch with your feelings, and give you tips on how to deal with stress.

- Set aside time to relax every day no matter what, and try not to be a perfectionist. The housework can wait; the phone can ring without you always answering it; and if the kids are screaming, then putting them to bed half an hour earlier so you can get some much needed relaxation isn't going to hurt. If you are tired, give yourself a break – you deserve it.

- As well as eating healthily to ensure your blood sugar levels are balanced and adrenaline production is controlled, make sure that you also exercise regularly. Exercise is a great way to de-stress. It stimulates circulation, improves digestion, and encourages your body and mind to get rid of toxins and stress.

- Take a multivitamin and multimineral supplement. The adrenals rely on Vitamin C, Vitamin B, zinc and magnesium to make hormones and function well, and these are rapidly decreased when you are under stress. If you are eating a healthy balanced diet with lots of fruit and vegetables and whole grains, you should be getting all the nutrients you need, but a good multivitamin and multimineral supplement every day makes sense as a back-up.

- Whenever you feel stressed or tense, practise the following breathing exercise to relax your body and mind:

– Breathe deeply and relax. For 2 or 3 minutes each hour, take a short mental vacation.

– You can engage in the following exercise while you are standing in the checkout queue at the supermarket or when listening to the other person talk while you are on the phone. You can then complete the exercise at home or at work. Take three deep breaths and relax. As you inhale, concentrate on calm and peaceful thoughts. You may think about relaxing by a mountain, by the ocean, or comfortably in your favourite room at home.

– As you exhale, concentrate on pushing any tension out of your lungs.

– Focus on positive images in your life. Focus on laughter, love, excitement and hope. If you cannot recall any of these things, imagine feeling happy and excited and hopeful.

– Keep breathing in and out in this way until you feel better. If you practise the exercise often enough, you will notice wonderful changes in your outlook and in other aspects of your life.

- Get a good night's sleep: this is essential to your health and well-being and your ability to cope with the stresses of daily life. Lack of sleep not only raises stress hormones, but research shows that it also interferes with blood sugar levels and increases your risk of depression. Unfortunately, sleep problems are a common symptom of depression, so it is a vicious circle. Getting quality sleep is easier said than done if you are suffering from depression but, as you will see below, there are things you can do to improve your chances of getting a good night's sleep.

Why can't I sleep?

Of all the symptoms of depression, insomnia can be the worst. It saps your physical strength, making it even more difficult to recover. People often wonder why depression causes insomnia. The answer lies in the fact that those with depression have a difficult time regulating the different mood and sleep hormones. The hormones you need to improve mood and energy are not the same ones you need to help you sleep.

For example, your body needs serotonin to be active and energetic during the day, but not at night, because this interferes with your ability to sleep. During the late evening and night, your body needs melatonin to help you pull back, withdraw and sleep. But high levels of melatonin in the daytime can cause you to feel lethargic, disoriented, irritable and moody. Often, depression is the result of your body producing the wrong hormones at the wrong time of day. The result: either you are wide awake in the middle of the night and can't keep your eyes open during the day, or you feel tired all the time and can't stop sleeping.

Improving your chances of a good night's sleep
First of all, boost your production of the hormone serotonin that promotes a good night's sleep by following the depression diet guidelines given previously. Eat foods that naturally boost your serotonin supply, such as lean meat, eggs, soya beans and low-fat dairy products, and make sure you are getting plenty of Vitamin B6 which is needed to boost the production of serotonin. Good sources of Vitamin B6 include spinach, lentils, carrots and fish. Bear in mind too that a deficiency of calcium and magnesium has been shown to cause sleeping problems, so try to include plenty of mineral-rich foods in your diet such as green leafy vegetables, nuts and seeds, and brown rice. Don't forget too to get plenty of exposure to daylight as daylight is essential for serotonin, so make sure you spend some time outdoors every day. Even if your mood and the day is overcast, your body and your mind will feel the benefits.

Move forward gradually

Having read the depression diet guidelines and the lifestyle advice to exercise regularly, watch your stress levels and get a good night's sleep, you should have a clearer idea of where changes need to be made in lifestyle as well as diet, and how these changes can help you beat depression. Remember, though, to take things slowly and move forward gradually so you don't feel overwhelmed.

Small and gradual change is the best way to create long-term improvement in your physical and emotional health. It can be tough at first when you don't feel better, but the advantage of taking things slowly is that it is more likely to have long-term results than quick-fix solutions. Think of it all as if it were a savings plans – if you look after the small things (in this case, the daily activities such as getting five a day of vegetables and fruit, eating more wholefoods and exercising for 30 minutes), then the big things (stress and depression) will look after themselves.

How much sleep do I need?

Everyone has different sleep needs, but if one or more of the items on the list below apply to you, you are not getting enough good-quality sleep:

- You yawn a lot.
- You fall asleep during the day.
- You lack energy.
- You feel drained or tired.
- You need caffeine and stimulants to get through the day.
- You get dark circles under your eyes.
- You find waking up difficult.
- You find it hard to concentrate.
- You get irritable for no reason.

But what is good-quality sleep? Up until recently, eight hours of sleep a night was recommended for optimum health, but it is important to realize that quality, not quantity, is the key when it comes to sleep. A recent study showed that a good night's sleep boosts health and well-being, but those who slept under six hours, or over seven hours, became irritable. While seven hours seems to be the most beneficial amount, six hours of good-quality sleep is far better than a restless eight.

The next step is to establish some good sleeping habits:

- Stick to a regular sleep–wake pattern, even at weekends. Ideally you should aim to be in bed at around 11 p.m. as studies show that people who sleep before midnight tend to wake more refreshed than those who go to bed in the small hours.
- Decide how much sleep you need. Eight hours is enough for most people, but you may need more or less than this to feel alert and refreshed. If you want to nap during the day, research shows that 25 minutes is the optimum time for a nap – longer than that and you will have trouble sleeping at night.
- Make sure your mattress and your bed are comfortable. Block out noise and light, as light will impair the production

of melatonin. Sleep in a well-ventilated, cool but not cold room (around 13–18°C/55–65°F) as body temperature naturally falls at night to promote feelings of sleepiness.

- Wind down for an hour or so before you go to bed. Activity delays melatonin production. Try taking a warm bath, doing yoga, having a quiet chat, making love, doing relaxation exercises, or drinking a cup of chamomile tea. If you can't sleep after lying in bed for more than half an hour, get up and do something monotonous – like reading or ironing. Then, when you feel sleepy, go to bed.

- It isn't wise to eat a heavy meal or drink a lot before going to bed. Stay away from the caffeine found in coffee, tea, chocolate and fizzy drinks. Alcohol isn't a good idea either. Besides disrupting your sleep, alcohol can also trigger symptoms of depression.

- Practise some relaxation techniques. Try lying on your back in bed, tensing every part of your body in turn and then relaxing it. This way, you can feel how good it is to be relaxed. You might want to do this with relaxing music playing.

- You might want to add aromatherapy oils, such as lavender or bergamot, to your bath. Or sprinkle a few drops of lavender essential oil on your pillow, or have a gentle massage with the oils. Herbs can help with sleep problems. Valerian, hops, passionflower, chamomile and skullcap all work as gentle sedatives and can improve the quality and duration of sleep.

- An hour before you go to bed, write a 'to do' list for tomorrow and put out the clothes you want to wear to stop you mulling over what you need to do and wear tomorrow.

- And if none of the above work, try not to get stressed out as the more you get anxious about not getting a good night's sleep, the less likely you are to sleep at all. The chances are that if you don't sleep well one night, you'll sleep like a log the next, especially if you are doing your daily exercise, getting plenty of fresh air, and following the depression diet guidelines.

7

A to Z of useful supplements for depression

Some experts believe that if you eat healthily all the time, you don't need supplements – but who eats healthily 100 per cent of the time?

If you are prone to depression, you can't afford to be deficient in any of the essential nutrients, as deficiency will make your symptoms worse; so on top of your depression diet you should consider taking a daily multivitamin and multimineral supplement containing Vitamins A, C, D, E and B1, B2, B5, B6, B12, plus folic acid, calcium, magnesium, iron, chromium, selenium and manganese.

In fact, studies[20] suggest that long-term vitamin and mineral supplementation can actually boost mood and brain power. The bulkiest nutrients are Vitamin C, calcium and magnesium, which are often inadequately supplied in a multivitamin and multimineral and may need to be taken separately.

Any herbs or dietary supplements you take in addition to your daily multivitamin and mineral should match your unique symptoms and needs. Remember that supplements are not a substitute for eating a healthy diet; they are a long-term insurance policy.

Caution: Large amounts of herbs and dietary supplements can be toxic and should only be taken under the guidance of a doctor or qualified nutritional consultant or herbalist. If you are on any medication, have high blood pressure, insulin resistance, are pregnant or hoping to be, you should take herbs and supplements only under the guidance of your doctor.

The supplements listed below in alphabetical order are those that research has shown to have a beneficial effect on people with depression.

Supplements A to Z

Amino acid therapy

Amino acids are what neurotransmitters are made of. In depression, the supplies of neurotransmitters in your brain are depleted. By supplementing your diet with the right amino acids, your brain can increase its production of neurotransmitters which results in an improved mood. Supplementation with the amino acids L-tyrosine[21] and D,L-phenylalanine[22] has in many cases been used as an alternative to antidepressant drugs. Another particularly effective treatment is the amino acid L-tryptophan. Additional research is needed to determine the optimal dosage and which types of patients are most likely to respond to treatment. Therefore amino acids should only be used as antidepressants under medical supervision.

Choline/lecithin

Choline accelerates the synthesis and release of the neurotransmitter acetylcholine, which is involved in many nerve and brain functions. Choline may be absorbed better in the form of lecithin. Choline supplements (in the form of lecithin) have been shown to bring some benefits in the treatment of bipolar disorder. The recommended supplement of choline is 500–800 mg.

Inositol

This is a naturally occurring substance involved in the production of certain brain chemicals. In a few studies, levels of inositol were lower in the cerebrospinal fluid (fluid surrounding the brain and spinal column) of depressed people compared to healthy people. Several small human studies[23] suggest that inositol may be of value in the treatment of depression, particularly for those who do not respond to antidepressant medications. More clinical trials are necessary to draw definitive conclusions on this substance, however.

Iron

Depression is often a symptom of chronic iron deficiency.[24] Other symptoms include general weakness, listlessness, exhaustion, lack of appetite and headaches. The recommended supplement for iron is 12 mg.

Magnesium

A deficiency of magnesium can cause numerous psychological changes, including depression. The symptoms of magnesium deficiency include poor attention, memory loss, fear, restlessness, insomnia, tics, cramps and dizziness. Plasma magnesium levels have been found to be significantly lower in depressed patients than in controls. Magnesium has also been used to treat premenstrual mood changes. These studies[25] suggest that magnesium deficiency may be a factor in some cases of depression. A nutritional supplement that contains 200–400 mg/day of magnesium may therefore improve mood in some patients with depression.

Omega-3 fatty acids

Essential fatty acids, such as omega-3 and omega-6 fatty acids, play a crucial role in the function of brain chemicals, particularly serotonin and dopamine. Studies[26] have shown that low levels of omega-3 fatty acids (found in cold-water fish such as tuna and salmon) may be associated with depression. The recommended dose of omega-3 fish oil supplements is 2–4 g daily. Vegetarians can take flax oil or hemp oil.

S-Adenosinemethionine (SAMe)

Some studies[27] suggest that the dietary supplement SAMe may be just as effective as tricyclic antidepressants for treating depression, but with fewer side effects. SAMe appears to boost serotonin levels in the brain, but further research investigating the mechanism of action (how it works), safety and effectiveness of SAMe for depression is warranted. Until more is understood, it is best to avoid using SAMe in conjunction with other antidepressants. Discuss its use with your healthcare provider who can help tailor your treatment accordingly.

Selenium

Some reports[28] indicate that the mineral selenium, found in wheatgerm, brewer's yeast, liver, fish, shellfish, garlic, sunflower seeds, brazil nuts and grains significantly affects mood. The recommended supplement for selenium is 55–70 mcg.

Tryptophan

This is an amino acid involved in the production of serotonin. Although some studies suggest that tryptophan depletion can lead to diminished serotonin levels and increase a person's susceptibility to depression, tryptophan use has been associated with the development of serious conditions such as liver and brain toxicity, and with a potentially fatal disorder that affects the skin, blood, muscles and organs. It is best to avoid this until more research has been done.

Vitamin B complex

The B-complex vitamins are essential to mental and emotional well-being. They cannot be stored in our bodies, so we depend entirely on our daily diet to supply them. B vitamins are destroyed by alcohol, refined sugars, nicotine and caffeine, so it is no surprise that many people may be deficient in these. The B vitamins work alongside one another, so it is better to take a Vitamin B complex rather than a specific B vitamin. Supplement with one 50 mg Vitamin B complex capsule daily.

Vitamin C and Vitamin E

Vitamin C may be valuable for patients with depression that is associated with low levels of serotonin. Some healthcare professionals recommend Vitamin C to reduce the symptom of dry mouth, a side effect experienced by many people taking antidepressant medications. Vitamin E may also be beneficial in treating depression. Both vitamins are powerful antioxidants[29] that seem to protect the brain against a variety of diseases. The recommended supplement for Vitamin C is 1,000 mg and 30 mg for Vitamin E.

Zinc

Inadequacies result in apathy, lack of appetite and lethargy.[30] If you don't think you are getting enough zinc in your diet, you may want to take a daily supplement of 15 mg.

Herbal remedies for depression

While many herbal remedies have been used traditionally to treat depression, the most substantial amount of scientific research has involved St John's wort.

St John's wort (Hypericum perforatum)

This is licensed as a standardized extract in Germany and other European countries as a treatment for mild to moderate depression, anxiety and sleep disorders. It appears to boost serotonin production. Over 20 clinical studies[31] have been completed using several different St John's wort extracts. Most have shown an antidepressant action either greater than placebo, or equal in action to standard prescription antidepressant drugs, but with fewer side effects.

The various B vitamins

Here is a rundown of recent findings[32] about the relationship of B-complex vitamins to depression:

- *Vitamin B1 (thiamine)*: The brain uses this vitamin to help convert glucose, or blood sugar, into fuel, and without it the brain rapidly runs out of energy. This can lead to fatigue, depression, irritability, anxiety, and even thoughts of suicide. Deficiencies can also cause memory problems, loss of appetite, insomnia and gastrointestinal disorders.[33] The consumption of refined carbohydrates, such as simple sugars, drains the body's Vitamin B1 supply.
- *Vitamin B3 (niacin)*: Pellagra – a condition which produces psychosis and dementia, among other symptoms – was eventually found to be caused by niacin deficiency. Many commercial food products now contain niacin, and pellagra has virtually disappeared. However, subclinical deficiencies of Vitamin B3 can produce agitation and anxiety, as well as mental and physical slowness.
- *Vitamin B5 (pantothenic acid)*: Symptoms of deficiency are fatigue, chronic stress and depression. Vitamin B5 is needed for hormone formation and the uptake of amino acids and the brain chemical acetylcholine, which combine to prevent certain types of depression.
- *Vitamin B6 (pyridoxine)*: This vitamin aids in the processing of amino acids, which are the building blocks of all proteins and some hormones. It is needed in the manufacture of

Dosage is typically based on hypericin concentration in the extract. There are many brands of St John's wort on the market and they can vary in strength and potency. The dose of 900 mg daily has been shown by studies to be effective in counteracting mild depression. Reported side effects include gastrointestinal complaints, fatigue, and oversensitivity to sunlight. Because of potential adverse interactions, St John's wort should not be taken in conjunction with other antidepressants or with certain medications, including indinivir (a protease inhibitor used for HIV), oral contraceptives, theophylline, warfarin, digoxin, reserpine, cyclosporine and loperamide.

serotonin, melatonin and dopamine. Vitamin B6 deficiencies, although very rare, cause impaired immunity, skin lesions and mental confusion.[34] A marginal deficiency sometimes occurs in alcoholics, patients with kidney failure, and women using oral contraceptives.

- *Folic acid*: Numerous studies[35] have linked a deficiency in folate with depression. Poor dietary habits contribute to folic acid deficiencies, as do illness, alcoholism and various drugs, including aspirin, birth control pills, barbiturates and anticonvulsants. It is usually administered along with Vitamin B12, since a B12 deficiency can mask a folic acid deficiency. Pregnant women are often advised to take this vitamin to prevent neural tube defects in the developing foetus.

- *Vitamin B12*: Because Vitamin B12 is important to red blood cell formation, deficiency leads to an oxygen-transport problem known as pernicious anaemia. This disorder can cause mood swings, paranoia, irritability, confusion, dementia, hallucinations or mania, eventually followed by loss of appetite, dizziness, weakness, shortage of breath, heart palpitations, diarrhoea and tingling sensations in the extremities.[36]

For suggestions on how to increase the amount of Vitamin B in your diet, refer back to Chapter 4.

Although they have yet to be scientifically evaluated and approved for their use in treating depression, the following are a few examples of herbs that may be recommended by professional herbalists for depression or its related symptoms:

Damiana

This may reduce the sexual dysfunction associated with many antidepressant medications.

Ginkgo biloba

This extract is considered helpful for elderly patients with depression as it appears to boost concentration and alertness. Depression is often an early sign of cognitive decline in elderly patients.

Siberian ginseng

Known as an adaptogenic herb (which means it adapts itself to individual needs), Siberian ginseng is believed to help the body adapt to stress – including the stress of fluctuating blood sugar levels.

Valerian root

This may help to improve symptoms of insomnia associated with depression.

8

Fine-tuning your diet to beat symptoms of depression

Not everyone with depression is the same. Following the depression diet and lifestyle detox guidelines will set you on the right path, but if you have a particular symptom or health problem along with depression, this can be a cause for special concern. In this chapter you'll see how you can add in adjustments, supplements and power foods either on their own or with other natural medicines to help you beat your particular symptoms.

Finding the diet boosters that can help ease the following:

For depression and anxiety, see page 70
For depression and apathy/low motivation, see page 72
For depression and fatigue, see page 72
For depression and digestive problems, see page 74
For depression and headaches/aches and pains, see page 76
For depression and insomnia/sleep disorders, see Chapter 6
For depression and loss of appetite, see page 78
For depression and loss of libido, see page 79
For depression and low mood/low self-esteem, see page 82
For depression and mood swings, see page 85
For depression and poor concentration, see page 88
For depression and weight gain, see page 90

Safety first

If you do decide to take herbs, make sure you do so under the care of a doctor who is familiar with herbal medicine. Inform your GP of all medicines, herbs and supplements you are taking – especially if you are on medication, have an existing health condition such as diabetes or high blood pressure, or are pregnant or hoping to be. If you decide to experiment with some of the natural therapies recommended in this chapter, always work with a skilled and qualified practitioner and let your doctor know what you are doing. Ideally your doctor could recommend a practitioner. And for more information on the supplements and/or herbs mentioned in this chapter, refer back to Chapter 7.

For depression and anxiety

Depressed people usually experience high levels of anxiety, and this can occur even if they have never had problems with anxiety before. Anxiety may be experienced as a persistent mood that lasts all day, not attached to any particular thought or situation (free-floating anxiety), or it may come and go as episodes of acute anxiety with panic attacks. In these attacks, the person experiences severe emotional and physical symptoms (such as sweating, shaking, upset stomach and shortness of breath) which may last for between 30 minutes and 2 hours, and which may be repeated frequently in a 24-hour period. Going to work, attending social gatherings, doing the shopping, or deciding what to wear may cause sufferers to become agitated, worried and distressed. This may become so bad that they avoid these situations altogether, possibly by spending the whole day in bed.

If anxiety levels are so high that they affect quality of life, it is important to seek medical advice. However, there are some simple diet and lifestyle changes and herbal treatments that can help ease some of the problems associated with anxiety.

When it comes to diet, it is well known that certain foods and substances tend to create additional stress and anxiety. Stimulants, such as caffeine found in coffee, tea, alcohol and fizzy drinks, and nicotine in cigarettes, stimulate an adrenal response in your body which can provoke anxiety, nervousness and insomnia to name just a few symptoms. Beware too of prescription drugs that contain caffeine and amphetamines, and recreational drugs such as cocaine that increase levels of anxiety and panic attacks in people using them.

Salt depletes the body of potassium, a mineral important to the proper functioning of the nervous system. Foods rich in potassium include raisins, apricots, sultanas and wheatgerm. Sweet refined foods should be avoided as these affect the blood sugar levels, which can lead to anxiety and mood swings. Additives and preservatives and monosodium glutamate (MSG) in Chinese takeaways are bad news as they can have a major irritating effect on the nervous system, producing the following: headaches, tingling, numbness and chest pains.

Anxiety has also been linked to a lack of folic acid. Food sources of folic acid include green leafy vegetables such as spinach, asparagus, cabbage and peas, but a folic acid supplement may also help.

Bear in mind too that stress and anxiety can be aggravated not only by what you eat, but the way you eat. Any of the following habits can aggravate your daily level of stress:

- Eating too fast or on the move.
- Not chewing food at least 15 to 20 times per mouthful.
- Eating too much to the point of feeling stuffed or bloated.
- Drinking too much fluid with a meal, which can dilute stomach acid and digestive enzymes (one cup with a meal is sufficient).

These behaviours put strain on your stomach and intestines in their attempt to properly digest and assimilate food.

Bear in mind that *how* you eat is important as well. Do make time to shop for food in a leisurely and enjoyable way, and to treat cooking as a creative or therapeutic activity where you can relax, knowing that you are doing the best you can to nourish yourself. Most importantly, take your time over actually eating the food. Eat when you are calm and relaxed, not when you are in a hurry or anxious. Give yourself permission to enjoy your food.

The depression diet is also the perfect diet for calming anxiety. Specific nutrients that are known to decrease anxiety include magnesium, Vitamin B complex and calcium. (Refer back to Chapter 4 for a list of food sources of these key nutrients.)

Some have found relief in the use of various herbal remedies for anxiety. Valerian is sometimes used for performance anxiety or in the treatment of insomnia. But some people find that this peps them up rather than relaxing them. California poppy has been shown to relieve mild anxiety and have some pain-relieving properties. Hops are also used for anxiety, restlessness and sleep disorders. They are also used in brewing beer. Passionflower has been shown to ease anxiety and insomnia caused by worry. Lemon balm not only sedates, but eases headaches related to tension. Lavender calms and relaxes most people. Chamomile not only relieves anxiety, but also helps to settle the stomach. Catnip relieves tension headaches and encourages sleep.

It is also important to carve out regular relaxation and time out for yourself. The stress management techniques in Chapter 6 can all help to ease anxiety. Meditation techniques such as focusing on your breathing can help to calm an anxious mind. Other relaxation rituals that may help include enjoying a cup of chamomile tea, massage, yoga or simply lighting a candle and relaxing in a warm bath. By making the time in your schedule for simple rituals such as these, you may find yourself less anxious and better able to deal with the daily stresses of life.

For depression and apathy

It is very common for a depressed person to lose interest in things that were previously a source of pleasure and enjoyment such as hobbies, sports, and other interests such as reading or watching films. Enjoyment in sexual activity is often lost, either in part, or completely. The person no longer feels any happiness or pleasure in life, and individuals may withdraw from a variety of activities because they see little point in continuing to do them or feel so tired and exhausted that they cannot muster the energy to start an activity.

Apathy or loss of pleasure in everyday things can affect you emotionally, mentally and physically and make you feel as if nothing is worth bothering about, including yourself. (For physical apathy, refer to the advice in this chapter on fatigue; for emotional apathy, refer to the advice here on low self-esteem and loss of libido; and for mental apathy, refer to the advice on poor concentration.)

When it comes to herbal supplements for apathy or low motivation, gingko biloba stands out head and shoulders above the rest. More evidence[37] exists for the beneficial effect of ginkgo biloba on mental function and alertness than for any other herb. It is said to improve memory, boost concentration, and sharpen mental focus in people of all ages.

For depression and fatigue

Depressed people generally experience low energy levels. They feel tired for much of the time and are easily fatigued. When you feel low, your energy is often sapped and feelings of listlessness and tiredness can take over. Wanting to stay in bed and sleep a lot is one of the signs of depression.

Diet has a big part to play in keeping fatigue at bay and avoiding slumps – which usually occur mid-morning and mid-afternoon. Following the depression diet guidelines and making sure you are eating plenty of fresh fruits and vegetables, whole grains such as brown rice and wholemeal bread, and quality protein such as soya, pulses and lean organic meat can all help. Avoid 'energy robbers' such as sugar, alcohol, fats, caffeine, white-flour products and highly processed foods. Eat less red meat and more lean meat and fish. Get enough energy-boosting zinc in your diet by eating plenty of nuts, seeds and fish. And make sure you get plenty of fibre too as constipation can deplete energy levels and drag you down.

Eating raw food is thought to boost energy levels. The argument is that over-cooking can destroy essential nutrients. Keep cooking to a minimum. Most foods only need to be simmered or steamed lightly. This doesn't mean you can't eat cooked food (in some cases cooking can enhance the nutrient content), it just means you should balance cooked food with raw. One of the best ways to achieve this balance between raw and cooked is to drink fruit and vegetable juices or smoothies on a daily basis.

Key energy-boosting nutrients include the antioxidants, calcium, magnesium, iron and zinc, but the most important energy foods are those rich in the B-complex group of vitamins. They are found in abundance in the whole grains of millet, buckwheat, rye, quinoa (a South American grain that is becoming more readily available), corn and barley.

If these grains are sprouted, their energy quotient is increased many times, as the enzyme action involved in the sprouting process increases the nutrient value. Sprouting is the process of soaking, then germinating, the seed and finally eating the growing live sprouts or sprinkling them on salads, adding them to juices, etc. The range of B vitamins is also to be found in fresh, green vegetables.

For a quick energy pick-me-up, sunflower seeds are packed with energy-boosting nutrients. They make a great snack and can be especially useful when it comes to that mid-morning or mid-afternoon slump. Wild blue green algae contains virtually every nutrient known to man, and if fatigue is a problem you might want to consider taking it in supplement form as it can provide a feeling of well-being, vigour and vitality.

The most popular herbal remedy for stress-related fatigue is ginseng. Supplementing with ginseng needs to be considered on an individual basis with a qualified practitioner, as there are different types.

Tips for more energy

- Get a good night's sleep.
- Start a gentle exercise routine. Even a ten-minute daily walk around the block can be energizing.
- If you are overweight, start to lose weight gradually. (See 'For depression and weight gain' on page 90.)
- Keep your sense of humour well stimulated. Spend more time with people who make you laugh, watch favourite comedies on television, even go to a pantomime if you like them.
- Sign up for some voluntary work to help people with a problem or cause that you feel strongly about.
- Dance or listen to upbeat music.
- Keep your creative thinking powers well stimulated. Play thinking games, read a good book, take up a new interest, hobby, learn a new language, join a debating society, or sign up for an evening class.
- Lime essential oil, lemon or peppermint in your morning bath can invigorate you.
- A cup of peppermint, lemon or ginger tea can help you feel more refreshed and awake.
- Experiment with therapies that are thought to boost energy, such as acupuncture, shiatsu, aromatherapy, yoga and massage.

For depression and digestive problems

Digestive problems, such as constipation, diarrhoea and irritable bowel syndrome (IBS), often occur alongside depression when the motivation to take care of yourself is low and the likelihood of unhealthy and erratic eating habits increases.

IBS in particular has been associated with depression, though experts say it is difficult to decide whether depression makes IBS worse, or is a result of the condition. Studies have repeatedly shown a higher incidence of depression in people with IBS, as well as higher levels of anxiety and hypochondria. Also, some of the medications used to treat depression may also relieve irritable bowel – for example, a selective serotonin reuptake inhibitor (SSRI) such as paroxetine. However, this needs a thorough evaluation from your doctor. If you are depressed, you may need higher doses of antidepressants than are commonly prescribed for IBS. Also, certain antidepressants can make some IBS symptoms worse, so it is important to get the right medicine for you as an individual. In addition, certain drugs, such as antibiotics, can alleviate the malabsorption problems of digestive disorders.

Having said this, dietary modification should be your first line of treatment. Healthy eating according to the depression diet guidelines, making sure you get enough fibre and drinking plenty of water, are the best solutions for digestive complaints.

Also watch out for food allergies and foods that trigger problems. The lactose found in milk and dairy products is a common culprit, and alcohol and tobacco can irritate the linings of the stomach and colon. When an intestinal upset occurs, make your diet blander than usual. Stick to alkaline foods such as fruit and vegetables and avoid acid-forming ones such as meat, fish, eggs, cheese, grains, bread, flour, sugar, peas, beans, legumes, tea, coffee, alcohol and milk.

Research has also found that people who practise stress management techniques have fewer and less severe attacks of IBS, and deep breathing exercises can help to relieve digestive complaints because shallow breathing reduces the oxygen available for proper bowel function. Chewing your food well and taking time when you eat, as well as avoiding food a few hours before bedtime, can also help.

Nettle tea, slippery elm tea, rhubarb root and other herbal formulas specifically designed for constipation can be found in your local health food stores. The best herb for IBS is thought to be gentiana root. Peppermint oil capsules can be helpful too.

Finally, 'food combining' can help with digestive disorders. Paying attention to the mix of alkaline-forming foods and acid-forming foods in every meal you eat might make it easier for your body to digest food and balance your intake. Be aware, though, that the original William Hay diet is very complex and rigid – go for more modern interpretations that explain it more simply.

IBS and depression – your four-point plan

1 Keep a symptom diary, noting when and where IBS symptoms occur, and how they make you feel. For example, factors that may play a part include types of food, how much food you eat, stress, medicines, your menstrual cycle, and your environment. If you regularly write down the types of foods you eat, when and where you ate them, the amount, and the symptoms associated with the food, it may help you work out what foods and situations trigger symptoms. For example, you may feel all right after eating one biscuit, but find that three makes you bloated, or that you enjoy a small slice of pineapple, but discover that a bowl of pineapple chunks is too much to cope with.

2 Increase your fibre intake. Fibre may be found in wholegrain bread and cereals, fruit, vegetables, and beans and legumes. Don't increase the level of fibre too much all at once, though – add a little more fibre every day to give your body time to get used to it. Do limit refined foods such as white bread, white rice, biscuits and so on.

3 Aim to drink eight glasses of water a day. Bear in mind that drinks such as coffee, carbonated drinks and alcohol have a dehydrating effect and can actually make your IBS worse.

4 Eat at leisure. As with other manifestations of depression and anxiety, it is too easy to make ourselves feel worse by eating 'on the hoof' or at our desks. Eating in such a rush reduces the pleasure you get from a meal, and can provoke IBS symptoms. While you are eating, try not to engage in other activities, such as driving, talking on the phone, or sitting in front of the computer. The stress may make you eat more quickly and swallow more air, causing gas or bloating or triggering other symptoms.

For depression and headaches/aches and pains

Aches and pains are very common in depression, and those with it often complain of generalized body aches. Or they may be concerned with a more localized type of pain – for example, headaches, chest pain or backache. Often, those with depression simply say that they feel pain all over and are unable to describe it very clearly. In the majority of cases, aches and pains are caused by the reduction of autonomic nervous system function that occurs in depressive illness.

Many factors can trigger headaches, aches and pains, and identifying them is an important part of treatment. A 'headache diary' used over a one- or two-month period can be used to identify triggers. You may find that a particular food, such as coffee, chocolate, onions, beans, cabbage, wheat, alcohol or red meat, or foods containing MSG, triggers an attack. You may also find that certain things, such as tight clothing, loud noises or the weather, are related to muscle aches and pains.

If your aches and pains are severe, you should see your doctor to discuss your options. Avoid a reliance on over-the-counter pain-killers because if you use them too often they lose their effectiveness. In less severe cases, the best way to prevent and control headaches and aches and pains is to eat little and often to keep blood sugar levels stable (low blood sugar can cause dilation of the blood vessels to the head), make sure that your diet is rich in magnesium (studies have linked magnesium deficiency to migraine attacks), and exercise regularly (it is believed that regular exercise can lessen the severity and occurrence of headaches). Stress management is also important as stress and muscle tension can trigger aches and pains.

A number of natural therapies have achieved some success for headaches and aches and pains generally. Massage can enhance circulation and relax the muscles. Acupuncture and aromatherapy may also be helpful, as may some herbal remedies, yoga and tai chi.

Aromatherapy

There are a number of different ways to use aromatherapy. Among the most effective application methods for headaches and aches and pains are the use of aromatherapy candles, the inhalation of oils and massage oils. Eucalyptus, lavender, tiger balm, peppermint and sandalwood applied to the forehead have proven to be particularly effective at combating migraines and other forms of headache.

Feverfew

This herb has recently become an incredibly popular method of combating headaches and, in particular, migraines. Feverfew acts as an anti-inflammatory and, as well as preventing the onset of migraines, it can also help to relieve feelings of nausea.

Passionflower (Passiflora)

This has gained a lot of respect in herbal medicine as providing a potential cure for various ailments. Among its uses, passionflower shows strong signs of relieving migraines and headaches, as well as lowering anxiety levels and working as an effective anti-inflammatory. This combination means that passionflower extracts can help to prevent the throbbing sensation in your head associated with cluster headaches and migraines.

Peppermint

This has several advantages as a headache and migraine cure. It tastes and smells pleasant and is easily obtainable. Clinical tests have also shown excellent results for many patients. Peppermint is best used as an essential oil, but you should avoid its consumption if you have acid indigestion or other digestive complaints.

Gingko biloba

These days, who *hasn't* heard of gingko biloba and its various uses as an herbal remedy? As well as being used to help alleviate headaches, it is also popular as an antidepressant and for improving memory and alertness. This unique combination of uses has made it extremely popular in health supplements and products for some years now.

For depression and insomnia/sleep disorders

Refer to the 'get a good night's sleep' advice in Chapter 6.

For depression and loss of appetite

The most common weight change seen in depressed people is weight loss that is not related to dieting, but is caused by a loss of appetite and a loss of interest in eating.

If possible, the first step in dealing with appetite loss is to treat the underlying cause. Treatment for conditions such as mouth sores, dry mouth, pain or depression should help to improve appetite.

Although you may not feel like eating, it is important to remember that good nutrition and maintaining a healthy weight are important parts of recovery from depression. Eating well can also help you to cope physically and emotionally.

The following tips may be useful in maintaining proper nutrition when your appetite is poor:

- Eat five to six small meals a day and snack whenever you are hungry.
- Determine what times of day you are hungry, make sure you eat at those times, and do not limit how much you eat.
- Avoid junk food and eat nutritious snacks that are high in calories and protein (for example, dried fruits, nuts, yogurt, cheeses, eggs, milkshakes, cereals and granola bars).
- Drink fluids between meals rather than with meals. Drinking during a meal can make you feel full too quickly.
- Choose nutritious drinks, such as milk, milkshakes and juices. Liquid protein drinks may also be helpful.
- Ask family members or friends to prepare foods when you are too tired to cook. Ask them to shop for groceries or buy pre-cooked meals.
- Try to eat in pleasant surroundings and to have your meals with family or friends.
- Eat food that is cold or at room temperature to decrease its odour and reduce its taste.
- Ask your doctor about ways to relieve other gastrointestinal symptoms such as nausea, vomiting and constipation.
- If your sense of taste is diminished, try adding spices and condiments to foods to make them more appealing.
- Try light exercise, such as a 20-minute walk, about an hour before meals to stimulate your appetite.

For depression and loss of libido

One of the most common symptoms of depression is loss of libido or loss of interest in things you normally enjoyed, such as hobbies, reading or watching films. In some cases, sexual dysfunction can be severe. Other problems include irregular or absent periods in women and impotence in men.

If your libido is low, the following tips may prove useful:

- Do eat healthily according to the guidelines in the depression diet. Vitamins A and B, and the minerals zinc and selenium, are all crucial for libido. And exercise helps too, by boosting your mood and body image.
- Check your stress levels. In general, stress dampens libido. Deal with commonplace stress by following the de-stressing tips on page 56.
- Most sex therapists agree that sex begins in the head – in a way, it is an idea that overtakes you. Your body's physical reaction follows. A key part of starting that sexual idea is setting the mood, and romantic music can help, as can low lighting, a candlelit bath, or your favourite romantic film. Once you are back in touch with your own desires, it can be easier and less daunting to connect with your partner's desires.
- Relationship troubles can also contribute to loss of sexual desire. If you don't feel listened to, respected or important, it is natural to respond with resentment – and that resentment can dampen libido. It is important to open the lines of communication with your partner so that anger can be expressed in places other than the bedroom. If the problem is severe, such as infidelity, you may want to go to a relationship counsellor.
- If you find the idea of sex unappealing or uncomfortable, talk to a sex therapist to discuss your health, your upbringing, your circumstances, any body image issues you may have, and your relationship, so that you can find ways to give yourself permission to satisfy your sexual needs. You may want to do this alone or you may find that it is more productive to talk to a sex therapist with your partner.
- If you feel you haven't got time for romance, make time. Give it a higher priority in your life. However busy or stressful your life gets, try to make sure that you have some 'couple time' where you can unwind together and talk about your day. And plan regular meals out, cinema trips, or weekend breaks so that the two of you get some special time together away from the hustle and bustle of your daily lives.
- Nature provides many safe, natural ways to boost sexual desire. Certain foods, such as chocolate, figs, ginger, oysters and nuts, are thought to contain aphrodisiac qualities because they contain nutrients that are essential for boosting libido.

Libido-boosting superfoods

Sauerkraut: This pickled cabbage contains enzymes to boost your health and sex drive and is good for the digestive system and liver. If you are eating poorly, your body is busy processing all the junk food and can't properly maintain the hormonal balance needed for enjoyable physical contact.

Strawberries: Eating strawberries and raspberries increases the sex drive of both men and women, according to a study conducted for British Summer Fruits in May 2004. This is due to the high levels of zinc found in the fruits' seeds which, unlike most fruits, are eaten rather than removed. Zinc is the most important nutrient for sexual function. It regulates sperm function, increases fertility, and heightens senses like taste and smell and makes for a better sex life. But it is not just the zinc content of the berry seeds that is beneficial in the bedroom. Strawberries are incredibly high in antioxidants which help to optimize blood flow to the sex organs, and they also have a low Glycaemic Index rating compared to other fruits, which means they provide sustained energy levels with only a few calories, so you can keep going for longer.

Hemp seeds: Hemp seeds are a rich source of several essential nutrients. In addition to containing vitamins and minerals, hemp seed, like the soya bean, is a vegetable source of complete protein, having all eight amino acids. Hemp seeds are a great way to get a healthy protein boost as, according to various studies, protein deficiency is linked not just to fatigue, weight gain and poor health, but also to low libido.

Pumpkin seeds: Bursting with nutrients that can boost prostate function, pumpkin seeds are also high in zinc, the mineral most associated with sex, libido and fertility.

Herbs to help with loss of libido

There are numerous herbal treatments that are thought to help put back sexual desire and drive into your life and these include agnus castus, black cohosh, damiana, dong quai, Siberian ginseng and wild yam for women, and saw palmetto, maca and horny goat weed for men. St John's wort can significantly boost sex drive in men and women who are depressed or physically exhausted, or for those whose loss of sex drive is linked to anxiety, stress, irritability or low mood. In one recent study,[38] 60 per cent of post-menopausal women who took St John's wort for three months said they found themselves feeling more sexy, and said that making love was more enjoyable. Wild oat (avena sativa) is often used for stress and fatigue, and is an ancient Chinese remedy for sexual decline. It is thought that oats can lower blood pressure and balance hormones[39] and therefore boost desire in men and women.

If you want to take herbs to boost your libido and/or to treat irregular periods or impotency, make sure you talk to a medical herbalist before self-prescribing.

Aromatherapy and libido

Aromatherapists believe that certain scents can have an aphrodisiac effect. Jasmine, rose, sandalwood and vanilla can be uplifting and sensual if used in the bath or as a massage oil, or dabbed on your pulse points. The sense of smell works through association too. Returning to a perfume you used to wear when you first met your partner may rekindle the passion. Massage with aromatherapy oils can also help to relax and invigorate you. Treat yourself to a massage or treat your partner to one.

For depression and low self-esteem

Depression is almost always associated with a profound loss of self-esteem and self-confidence. The depressed person no longer feels in control of his/her life, and things that were accomplished easily before may now seem impossibly difficult. A depressed mood also leads the person to look at everything in a black, negative and pessimistic light. Although those who are depressed may be functioning at a reasonable level, they tend to be very self-critical and are unable to acknowledge that they can do anything well. They are unreasonably tough on themselves and view all that they do as a failure.

If people have never experienced depression before, they may be quite unable to recognize that what is happening to them is actually an *illness*. They may blame themselves for the problems they are having and tell themselves they are not trying hard enough. Relatives and friends may do the same, adding further comments about 'pulling your socks' up. This sort of moralizing talk just makes matters worse.

Low self-esteem can gradually destroy the quality of your life and push you towards full-blown depression. You start to take less and less care of yourself. Your relationships, your sex life and your work suffer. You sell yourself short by deciding that you aren't good enough before you even start something, which means you don't put the effort in and end up by confirming to yourself your view that you have no worth. It has been said many times before, but thinking positively and putting more emphasis on the good things in your life is a great way to build up your self-esteem. No one says this is easy, but here are a few ideas to get you thinking along the right lines:

Think and talk in a new language

Negative feelings do not actually result from the bad things that happen to you, but from the way you think about these events. If you think and talk negatively or always put yourself down, then sooner or later you will end up believing those thoughts. A powerful self-esteem booster is to make an effort to fill your thoughts and language with positive, liberating messages. For instance, avoid saying 'I can't' or 'I'm useless' and replace it with something like 'I'll try my best' or 'I am getting better'. If this makes sense to you, you might well benefit from cognitive behaviour therapy (CBT), which uses these kinds of techniques to banish negative self-talk.

The glass is half full

Turn problems into challenges, and fear into excitement. Avoid 'should' and 'ought' and replace with 'could'. When something goes wrong, remember to put it into perspective. It is one event and it doesn't mean that you will always get it wrong. Don't think to yourself 'I've failed', think 'I'm learning new things all the time and I'll know better next time'. Don't think 'I'm depressed and am always going to feel this way'. Instead, try to think 'Depression is encouraging me to reassess my life and what is important to me so that I can move forward more positively'.

Smile more

You are bound to feel better when you do this. It is all too easy to get stuck in a complaining rut and focus on the down and serious side of life. Make room for some playtime, whether it's watching your favourite comedy, spending time with a friend who always lifts your spirits, or reading your favourite book. And smile more, even if you don't feel like it. Smiling can help to stop you feeling bad about yourself and encourage others to communicate with you. If you don't feel like smiling, force yourself – you've got nothing to lose and everything to gain.

Teach others how to treat you

If people aren't valuing you it is because you are letting them. Ask yourself why you are allowing this to happen and change the relationship by changing your behaviour. If you act assertively, people who treat you like a doormat will either change their behaviour or leave your life. An assertive person knows what she wants and respects her own wishes; she believes she can make things happen and does them; she isn't afraid to say no or take a chance; she accepts responsibility for her actions, expresses her true feelings, and respects and values the feelings of others. Above all, though, she values herself.

Do something

If you've been promising yourself that you'll learn a new language, start a new course, decorate your room, get a new wardrobe or style makeover, phone your parents, clean the house or take a holiday, make sure you stop procrastinating and *do* it. Even if you don't feel like it, don't put your life on hold any longer and get started. Try doing something creative like painting a picture or writing a letter or baking a cake. It is amazing how quickly our interest in life can be recaptured when we encourage ourselves to be creative. And why not do something you have never done before? Encourage your natural curiosity – it may be a concert, an activity, a trip or a class. When we do something for the first time we always experience a charge of energy and learn new things about ourselves.

Get into the habit of self-confidence

Self-confidence is your birthright – just look at any newborn baby; it wants and expects love. Lack of self-confidence is something that has happened to you along the way and become a habit – perhaps because of negative messages that were given to you. Break that habit and replace it with the habit of self-confidence. After all, it is your right. If you don't feel very confident, pretend to be; most of us do that all the time and, just as with smiling, the act of pretending will push you in the right direction.

Be your own best friend

If your friend or partner had done something well you would want to reward them, so do it for yourself too. The next time you feel pleased with yourself because you've done something well, reward yourself with a treat, a trip, a meal or some leisure time. If you don't think you do anything well, then spend some time focusing on your strengths. Write out a list of all the things you know you are good at – from dealing with people to making a chocolate cake, or being on time. You will be surprised at the lift it gives you when you concentrate on your positive strengths. When you feel really low, try this wonderful technique to lift you out of your negativity. Imagine that you have stepped out of your body and are standing next to yourself. Become your own best friend. Now, what would you say to yourself that is comforting and helpful? How can you encourage this person to feel more confident about herself? What would you say to your best friend? Perhaps you would put your arm around her and tell her that she is doing really well and that you appreciate all the good things about her. Talk to yourself the way you would to your best friend.

Take care of yourself

Last but by no means least, take care of yourself by following the depression diet guidelines in this book. Making such positive changes will do wonders for your self-esteem as it encourages you to respect yourself and give your body and mind only the best. (If you find it hard to give yourself the best, refer to Chapter 10.)

For depression and mood swings

In women, mood swings or periods of irritability and/or restlessness are often related to hormonal fluctuations and may occur before the monthly period, during and right after pregnancy, and during the menopause. But female hormones aren't the only culprits: men, too, can get mood swings.

The natural remedies below, used with the approval of your doctor, may help to control mood swings, according to some health professionals:

- Cut out sugar. Mood swings may be related to an overgrowth of yeast in the intestines. Yeast may also develop after consuming certain trigger foods, such as refined sugar. If you are prone to mood swings, limit your intake of yeast-producing foods such as vinegar and refined and processed products, as well as refined sugar, caffeine and alcohol. Mood swings can also be caused by foods that typically cause allergic reactions in people – things such as milk products and wheat, so if you notice mood swings after consuming these foods, you might have a food allergy and should avoid them.
- Irritability has been linked to a lack of Vitamin B6, found in whole grains and bananas; magnesium, found in vegetables, nuts and seeds; and selenium, found in fish, garlic and sunflower seeds. Make sure too that your multivitamin and multimineral supplement contains enough of these important nutrients.
- Hydrotherapy. The next time you need to 'chill out', fill your bath with water that is just slightly cooler than body temperature. It should feel like a hot bath that is beginning to get a little chilly. Soak for 20 minutes, adding water as needed to maintain the temperature of the bath.
- Sound therapy. Mood swings often arise because of stress, anger or anxiety. Some people find relief from shifting moods by listening to relaxing music with a slow, steady beat, which slows your heart rate and calms your mind. Try listening to this type of music for about 30 minutes a day. Here's another idea: if you live near the sea, try sitting on or near the beach for half an hour or so each day. Ocean waves crash the shore at a steady rhythm that helps to calm you down. If you can't get near the sea, buy (or make) a cassette or CD of ocean waves. It's probably not quite as good as the real thing, but the rhythm will still be the same.

Managing anger

If you find that your mood swings or outbursts are negatively affecting your relationships with family, friends, co-workers and even complete strangers, it is probably time to change the way you express your anger. Here are some tips to get your moods and your anger under control:

- Take a 'time out'. Count to 10 before reacting or leave the situation altogether. If you are very angry, count to 100.

- Do something physically exerting when you feel angry or low. Physical activity can provide an outlet for your emotions, especially if you are about to erupt. Go for a walk or a run, swim, lift weights or use a punch bag, for example.
- Find ways to calm and soothe yourself. Practise deep-breathing exercises, visualize a relaxing scene, or repeat a calming word or phrase to yourself, such as 'take it easy'. You can also paint, write or do yoga.
- Express your anger as soon as possible so that you aren't left stewing. If you can't express your anger in a controlled manner to the person who has made you angry, try talking to a member of your family, a friend, counsellor or another trusted person.
- Use 'I' statements when describing the problem to avoid criticizing or placing blame. For instance, say 'I'm upset you didn't help with the housework this evening' instead of 'You should have helped with the housework this evening'. To do the latter is likely to upset the other person and escalate tensions.
- Don't hold a grudge. Forgive the other person. It is unrealistic to expect everyone to behave exactly as you want.
- Use humour to defuse your anger, such as imagining yourself or the other person in silly situations. Don't use sarcasm, though – it's just another form of unhealthy expression.
- Keep an 'anger log' to identify the kinds of situations that set you off and to monitor your reactions.

You may need to keep something with you that serves as a reminder to step back from the situation and get your anger under control. For instance, you may want to keep a small, smooth stone in your pocket or a scrap of paper with your tips written down on it. With repetition, these anger management techniques will come more naturally and you will no longer need such physical reminders.

Finally, mood swings may mean that you have lost balance in your life and are feeling stressed, so refer also to the stress management tips in Chapter 6. If your mood swings are unpredictable and uncontrollable or your moods alternate between intense joy and deep despair, consult your doctor immediately. You might benefit from anger management sessions. You might even be suffering from bipolar disorder and treatment will offer relief.

For depression and poor concentration

Depression may cause marked changes in your mental ability as it relates to concentration, attention and memory. Concentration is most often affected. Depressed people may find that they can no longer do tasks requiring much attention for any length of time (such as watching a television programme until the end or reading for lengthy periods). They may only be able to do something for a short period of time, sometimes only minutes, before they feel distracted or need to stop.

Memory and decision-making are also commonly affected by depression and seem to worsen the more severe the depression becomes. This can cause problems. The depressed person seems absent-minded, indecisive and forgetful, and this helps further to increase feelings of frustration and inadequacy.

Experts agree that your memory is like a muscle; the less it is used, the more quickly it atrophies. If you do the same thing day in and day out – what is commonly known as being in a rut – your mind won't get the workout it needs to stay sharp, regardless of your age. The natural remedies below may help improve your memory but, as always, if your concentration problems are causing severe problems, consult your GP:

- *Watch your fats*: Memory problems are often caused by poor blood flow. Making sure you are avoiding unhealthy fats and eating quality fats will help open up arteries and improve blood flow. Refer to the healthy fats guidelines on page 42.
- *Specific nutrients*: The nutrients thought to boost memory include: omega-3, found in fish, nuts and seeds; Vitamin B5, found in whole grains and vegetables; Vitamin B6, found in whole grains and bananas; and Vitamin B12, found in fish and eggs. Specific nutrients thought to boost concentration include: Vitamin B1, found in whole grains and vegetables; Vitamin B12, found in lean meat and low-fat dairy foods; and zinc, found in seafood and nuts.
- *Gingko biloba*: The herb ginkgo biloba may help to reverse memory loss caused by poor circulation to the brain, but you need to take it for one to three months before you notice improvements. Studies demonstrate that ginkgo biloba exerts a direct effect on mental alertness by increasing blood flow to the brain and modifying the frequency of brain waves associated with alertness

Depression and poor concentration – try the 'Mozart effect'
Poor concentration is one of the most upsetting things about having depression. However, some research indicates that listening to music you enjoy may stimulate areas of your brain and boost your concentration. Even humming to yourself is thought to have positive benefits. The 'Mozart effect' stems from work done in 1993 by psychologist Frances Rauscher, of the University of Wisconsin at Oshkosh, and her colleagues. They discovered that listening to Mozart improved people's mathematical and spatial reasoning compared with, say, listening to white noise or music by the minimalist composer Philip Glass.

This theory has since been questioned, and some researchers feel that music boosts brain power simply because it makes listeners feel better – both relaxed and stimulated. Indeed, one study found that listening to a story gave a similar brain boost.

There is more evidence that actually learning to play an instrument may help to boost brain power. Rauscher found that after two years of music lessons, pre-school children scored better on spatial reasoning tests than those who took computer lessons.

Maybe music lessons exercise a range of mental skills, with their requirement for delicate and precise finger movements, and listening for pitch and rhythm, all combined with an emotional dimension. Nobody knows for sure. Neither do they know whether adults can get the same mental boost as young children.

However, some researchers believe the effect is not limited to Mozart or other classical composers, but may stray over a wide range of genres, including samba, waltz, Native American and African rhythms, and even rock and roll. Several studies conclude that even our own voices can help, showing that people who sang to themselves or even just hummed a tune needed fewer or no painkillers after certain types of surgery. Many migraine sufferers also use humming as a way of preventing attacks or reducing the use of medication.

So, while the controversial Mozart effect may not be fully proven yet, one thing is certain: listening to music that makes you personally feel relaxed and energized can only help you get the best out of your depression diet. Try putting some music on during your next meal so you enjoy every mouthful.

(alpha rhythms) and decreasing the brain waves associated with lack of attention (theta rhythms).

- *Do something new*: Shake your brain out of its routine by doing something new. Go to work via a different route, brush your teeth with a different hand, sit in a different chair to the one you normally use, and so on. The more you challenge and stimulate your brain, the more alert it remains.

Use it or lose it

Although yoga and meditation are also thought to improve memory and concentration, perhaps the best way to boost your brain power is to think more. Your mind is like a muscle. The more you use it, the stronger and more efficient it becomes. Try to stimulate your brain every day with mental challenges such as crosswords, puzzles or thinking games such as chess. Switch the television off and read instead. Visit an art gallery, learn a new language, take up a new hobby, or join a debating society or book group. Your brain thrives on such stimulation; you might even enjoy it too.

For depression and weight gain

Comfort eating is a familiar phenomenon for some depressed people (see Chapter 9). Depression may increase your appetite for sweet, rich foods to boost your mood but, as seen previously, such foods have the opposite effect because they cause rapid fluctuations in blood sugar levels which trigger depression and weight gain. One simple ploy is to get out into the daylight more – without glasses if you wear them (see the section on SAD on page 53).

You will find some effective weight-loss strategies below. If your weight gain is due to comfort eating and/or food cravings, refer first to the section in Chapter 9 about healing your emotional relationship with food. If your weight gain is due to unhealthy eating habits, refer to Chapter 9.

Depression-relief weight-loss strategies

Follow the depression diet guidelines and you may find that you lose weight naturally after one to three months, especially if you are exercising regularly too. If you don't lose any weight after three months or so, one of the most effective ways to lose it is by portion control. You don't need to cut out your favourite dishes – you just need to eat less of them. If you think that smaller portions won't satisfy your hunger, there are things you can do to give you that full feeling:

- Take time over your meals. Put your knife and fork down after each mouthful and chew food slowly.
- If you think you need to eat more, wait 10–15 minutes to see if you are still hungry. It takes quite a while for your brain to recognize when your stomach is full.
- Never shop or cook when you are hungry. Keep a supply of healthy, low-fat, low-sugar snacks nearby, such as apple and nuts, dried fruit and low-fat yogurt, so you never get really hungry.
- It takes time for your stomach to adjust to smaller portion sizes, so give yourself time and make sure you follow the little-and-often rule. Around six small meals a day is best for losing weight and for keeping hunger at bay. If there is a long gap between meals, blood sugar levels fall too low, leaving you tired, craving sugar, and lacking in energy and concentration. Give your body food every few hours to boost your metabolic rate and keep blood sugar levels stable.
- Stop eating several hours before you go to bed, say at 8 p.m. A light snack, perhaps a cracker and a glass of low-fat milk, is OK if you feel peckish, but not a heavy meal. This is because your body needs to rest, not digest, when you sleep. It doesn't make sense to eat lots of food when all you are going to do is sleep. The earlier in the day you eat, the more likely you are to burn off calories, even if you aren't active.
- Make nutrient-rich foods such as whole grains, fruits and vegetables the staples of your diet. They are filling, but low in calories.
- Drink a glass of water before you eat to make you feel fuller and flush out toxins. Water can also have a direct impact on energy; we may reach for a sugar fix when what we really need to do is drink something and rehydrate.
- Having a bowl of soup may also help you lose weight. US researchers at Johns Hopkins University in Baltimore found that people who chose soup as a starter consumed 25 per cent less fat in the main course that followed.

- All nutrients are important when it comes to weight loss, but some are more important than others. If you are deficient in B vitamins, Vitamin C, calcium, manganese, magnesium, zinc, essential fatty acids (for food sources, see Chapter 4), chromium found in whole grains, bananas, carrots, cabbage, mushrooms and strawberries or co-enzyme Q10 which is found in sardines, whole grains and mackerel, this could hinder your weight loss plans as these nutrients are vital for metabolism and controlling your appetite and blood sugar levels. (Fluctuating blood sugar levels don't just trigger depression, they can also trigger weight gain.)
- A good night's sleep is important as lack of sleep slows your metabolism and increases your risk of over-eating and weight gain.
- Some studies suggest that drinking green tea may aid weight loss as it contains antioxidant compounds that could increase your metabolism.
- When it comes to herbal boosters for weight loss, supplements such as Siberian ginseng, fennel, cinnamon or fenugreek may help, but you need to make sure you consult your doctor and a trained dietician first. Certain herbal supplements can be toxic in large doses. And unless your doctor feels that your weight carries a serious risk to your health, steer clear of slimming drugs of any kind. What you need is permanent weight loss: the drawback of slimming drugs is that they are like diets – they slow down your metabolism and never work in the long term.

9

'Eating your emotions'

We all do it – reach for something that unequivocally feels good to eat when we are low. But if you continually comfort-eat whenever you feel low, stressed or depressed, you may find it hard to stick to the depression diet guidelines. That is why this chapter focuses on healing your emotional relationship with food. If you haven't got a positive relationship with food, you are putting yourself under too much pressure and simply setting yourself up for disappointment.

Comfort-eating

Do you ever reach for a comforting chocolate bar when you need to calm down, hope that an extra-strong coffee will perk you up, or rely on junk food to boost your energy? If so, you are not alone – junk food is often the first thing that people reach for in depression.

Major life events such as unemployment, health problems, divorce and a shortage of emotional support and daily-life hassles such as a difficult commute to work, bad weather, and changes in your normal routine are thought to trigger emotional eating. But why do negative emotions lead to overeating?

How your body reacts to mood and food may play a role. Research indicates that some foods, in particular fatty and sugary ones, might have seemingly addictive qualities for many people. When you eat palatable foods such as chocolate, your body releases trace amounts of mood- and satisfaction-elevating opiates. That 'reward' may reinforce a preference for foods that are most closely associated with specific feelings.

There is a reason why comfort-eating foods are often sugary and fatty, and that is because these foods can boost serotonin (also called endorphins) production – the 'feel good' brain chemical we have already looked at. The trouble is, as we have also seen previously, if you comfort-eat with high-sugar foods, you will end up with an endorphin rush, fluctuating sugar levels, and slumps in energy and mood. This leaves you feeling worse than you did before, and the chances are you will reach for another sugary fix to lift you – thus repeating the vicious cycle all over again.

From a mental standpoint, food can also be a distraction. If you are worried about an upcoming event, or rethinking a conflict from earlier in the day, or just feeling bored, eating comfort foods may distract you. But the distraction is only temporary. While you are eating, your thoughts may be focused on the pleasant taste of your comfort food. Unfortunately, when you have finished overeating, your attention returns to your worries – and you may now bear the additional burden of feeling guilty about your overeating.

If you find yourself turning to food for comfort on a regular basis or think that your relationship with food is making it hard for you to eat healthily, it is vital that you understand the link between food and mood so that you can move towards a healthier way of eating and living.

Disordered eating

Comfort-eating isn't only going to make you feel worse, it is dangerous – as it can make you more vulnerable to eating disorders, such as anorexia, bulimia or disordered eating patterns. If you reach for food whenever you feel unhappy, there is a risk that you may become bulimic and binge on massive amounts of food and then vomit or use laxatives afterwards to rid yourself of it. Between binges you may go on strict diets, even starving yourself, which could set you on the way to developing anorexia.

Any eating pattern that is taken to the extreme is dangerous. Your body does not get the nutrients it needs to keep you feeling healthy and happy, bingeing and starving trigger blood sugar imbalances, and the hormonal havoc this causes can make your depression worse.

There is a well-documented link between comfort-eating, eating disorders and depression. Eating disorders are, however, such a complex and dangerous health concern that they are outside the scope of this book. Needless to say, it is crucial that if you suspect that you have an eating disorder, you ask your doctor for help and advice.

You may not think about food all the time and have a full-blown eating disorder like anorexia and bulimia, but still have an unhealthy attitude towards food and think about food more than is considered normal. Perhaps you are constantly dieting or switching from one exercise fad to another. If this is the case, in the long run it is just as damaging to your health and well-being as the full-blown eating disorder. You won't be getting the nutrients you need to balance your hormones and your blood sugar, and this can cause or trigger depression. You will also be increasing your risk of diabetes, heart disease, infertility and obesity. And weight loss will be harder because unhealthy eating confuses your metabolic rate, so that when you do eat, you store as fat a greater proportion of what you consume.

If you are depressed and start to binge, fast, diet or yo-yo diet, not only will this make it impossible for you to eat healthily, it will create nutritional deficiencies and make your depression worse. If you feel that your eating patterns are spiralling out of control and the quality of your life is being affected, the advice and information in this book can certainly help, but it is still crucial that you seek advice from a doctor or dietician immediately.

Restoring and healing your relationship with food

So if comfort-eating in response to low moods and stress is ruining your chances of success, what should you do?

First of all, you need to get your relationship with food on track and it's best to do this before you start making any changes to your diet. Your doctor can put you in touch with a dietician if you think this will be useful, or help you find a counsellor who specializes in eating problems. You can get support from eating disorder organizations and websites. If you don't want to ask your doctor for this kind of help, you can do some research yourself to find a suitable counsellor.

You may also find these 'building a healthy relationship with food tips' helpful:

- Don't ban certain foods from your diet. If you ban a food, it just makes it worse – all you do is think about it. (If someone says to you 'Don't think about a cup of delicious hot chocolate with whipped cream', what's the first image that pops into your head?) Food in itself isn't your enemy. You shouldn't feel guilty when you eat a particular food – you just need to learn how to choose wisely the foods that you do eat. There really is no such thing as an unhealthy food, only an unhealthy attitude towards food. If you can change your attitude to food, you can eat healthily without feeling deprived and also allow yourself the occasional indulgence without feeling guilty.

- If thinking about food makes you anxious, one of the best techniques is relaxation. Find other ways to ease the tension rather than reaching for the fridge door. There are many different ways to relax, and you need to find out what works best for you. Taking deep, slow breaths, gently clenching and relaxing your muscles, phoning a friend, going for a walk, or simply listening to your favourite music are just some of the many tried and tested ways to clear your mind and ease tension.

- Meditation for ten or so minutes twice a day can help to keep food cravings at bay – perhaps because it shuts off your mind and allows you to relax. You don't need to join a class – just sit upright, close your eyes, and focus on your breathing. If thoughts about food intrude, just let them go as if your thoughts are grains of sand running through your fingers.

- Wait 20 minutes after you eat a meal or snack before eating more. It takes at least 20 minutes after a meal for your brain to register that your stomach is full. This is especially important if you always feel hungry after eating. Feeling full is not an instantaneous signal.

- Don't place any unnecessary food regulations on yourself as this is edging dangerously close to a full-blown eating disorder. If you really can't resist a food, take three bites and then give or throw the rest away. The first bite is heavenly bliss so really taste and enjoy it, let the food linger in your mouth. Thoroughly enjoy the second bite too. Let the third bite emotionally register that you had the opportunity to eat a wonderful food and then get rid of it, letting go of any feelings of resentment and punishment that you might have had if you had denied it to yourself.

- When you do eat, remind your brain that you are doing so. Focus on your food. Turn off the television during meals and don't read when you eat. Always sit down to eat, and put your knife and fork down between each mouthful so that you can savour and enjoy your food properly. Make eating a memorable occasion. Lay the table, use a tablecloth, decorate your table, and use your best dishes. What are you saving them for? All of these food memory joggers are especially important when you are eating alone, or eating when you are tired after a busy day.

- Become more aware of your feelings when you eat. Are you eating because you are hungry, or because you feel sad, angry or frightened? You may find that a food and mood diary where you write down what you eat, when you eat, and how you feel before, during and after eating, can help. This isn't to help you control your food intake, but to help you to understand your eating habits and to recognize what triggers the need to comfort-eat. If comfort-eating has become a habit, you may have lost the ability to judge when you are really hungry.

- Not being able to recognize true hunger signals often stems from not focusing fully on eating. If you aren't focusing on your food and just popping food in without thinking about it, you don't notice when you are full. The next time you want to eat, ask yourself if you are really hungry. If you aren't sure, your probably aren't. Ask yourself if something other than food, like a walk, a hug or a chat, would satisfy you instead.

- If you think you are hungry, a useful tip is to drink a glass of water as thirst often gets confused with hunger. And try smelling your food before you eat it. Smell is the sense most directly linked to the brain and it is your sense of smell that will help you to get in touch with what your body needs. Does the hamburger you lusted after smell as good as it looks? Probably not.

- Focus your thoughts on how healthy eating can make you feel and look better. The next time you are tempted to eat something that you know is going to lead to poor health, weight gain and depression, ask yourself if you could really enjoy it. You may think that you are treating yourself when you comfort-eat, but if it leads to weight gain and a worsening of your symptoms, is that really a treat?

- If you do comfort-eat on a regular basis, your self-esteem could be fairly low and this will have a negative impact on eating habits. If you often feel bad about yourself and reach for food as comfort, this can be a hard habit to break out of. It also stops you taking good care of yourself. The first thing you need to understand is that you are an OK person and you deserve the best – and that includes eating the best. Also helpful are positive statements you repeat to yourself over and over again until they sink in, such as 'I feel confident' or 'I can do this'. Remind yourself too that you have a right to be assertive, to express your opinions and emotions, and to be the unique individual you are. Just because you feel down doesn't make you any less of a person. You have the right to make mistakes and change your mind, just like everyone else. There will be times when you eat things that aren't good for you. It is not a big deal. You can start eating healthily tomorrow.

- Other tips for building self-esteem include giving yourself lots of non-food treats, especially when things are stressful – such as a soothing massage, a new haircut or outfit, going to the theatre, or curling up with a good book, giving yourself quality time to chill out and enjoy your own company, saying 'no' more often, getting support from loved ones and people who make you feel good about yourself and last, but by no means least, being yourself and making sure your goals are what *you* want – not what your partner, your family or your friends want.
- The tips given below on stress-proofing your diet, and dealing with sugar cravings, can also help.

Stress-proofing your diet

Stress-proofing your diet will help you at those times when you know you are most vulnerable, and when you need to adapt your eating to the daily stresses of life such as work deadlines, rush hour, no time to cook, family dinners, and so on:

- Plan ahead with a daily eating and exercise schedule, and know what you are going to eat for your snacks and main meals, and when you are going to take your exercise. Without planning, you will be likely to skimp on your exercise and make yourself vulnerable to unhealthy eating, especially at the most trying time for comfort-eaters – 3 p.m. to midnight. Knowing what you are going to eat and how you are going to plan your day beforehand will limit uncertainty and guilt and make things easier and less stressful in the long run.
- If you are eating out, there is no need to worry – just pay attention to what you are ordering. If you make healthy food choices on the menu, stay away from the bread basket, drink lots of water instead of fizzy or alcoholic drinks, go for lots of soup and salad, tomato or wine-based sauces rather than cheese-based or buttery ones, and ask for dressings on the side, then you should be fine. And when it comes to dessert, go for fruit or try the 'three bites' technique we suggested earlier.

- Keep lots of healthy snacks nearby in your fridge, car or desk so they are there when you need them and you don't have to rush to the chocolate vending machine.
- Don't skip breakfast. If you do, you will eat too much later in the day. And make sure you have a mid-morning snack about three hours after breakfast – ideally some protein, like yogurt, and a piece of fruit. Eat your mid-afternoon snack about three hours after lunch. This should include protein and carbohydrate and be low in fat. For example, soup with crackers, cottage cheese and fruit, and so on. And finally try to eat most of your calories before 5 p.m. and don't eat too much after 8 p.m. as your body is geared up for rest then, not digestion.
- If you really, really crave a sweet food, treat yourself with it now and again – you don't have to ban it completely. An occasional chocolate bar, white bread, cake or glass of wine won't hurt you. Go ahead and really enjoy it – remember the 80/20 rule we mentioned in Chapter 3. The same applies to cooking – don't beat yourself up if once in a while you have a ready-prepared meal, when you know that cooking would make you feel tired and stressed.
- Keep cooking simple. Many comforting dishes are actually easy to prepare and they don't have to be unhealthy: soup with beans, for example, or baked apples with raisins, or low-fat cheese on toast – all of these are simple, but delicious and nutritious. Eating should be a source of pleasure. The last thing you want to do is make it a source of stress.
- Sometimes, however much we plan ahead for stress, things change and eating routines have to adapt quickly. Keep your cupboards, fridge and freezer well stocked with emergency healthy foods such as soup, beans, canned vegetables and low-fat frozen meals. Chopped fresh fruit and vegetables make great sandwich fillers and are good to nibble on when you feel hungry. If your routine is totally disrupted – for example, the kitchen is flooding or you are moving house – keep as active as you can and help yourself to fruit, vegetables and wholegrain bread sandwiches rather than high-fat alternatives.
- Don't forget the healing power of exercise during times of stress. It can lift your mood because it makes your body produce endorphins. It can help you lose weight by speeding up your metabolism and distracting you from food. It can help manage

your stress hormones and give you feelings of pleasure and control in situations where you feel helpless and out of control. So the next time you crave food because you are feeling low, go outside for a brisk walk instead.

Addicted to sugar

Susan, who we met in Chapter 1, became quite dependent on sugar from her teenage years onwards, both in edible form and in alcohol. If you find the sugar habit incredibly hard to break, the best remedy is to make sure you are getting enough quality protein and fat as they slow down the release of sugar into your bloodstream. You also need to eat little and often and watch the Glycaemic Index when making food choices. Chromium supplements may also help you control sugar cravings as studies have shown that people with blood sugar problems often have a chromium deficiency. The organic, chelated forms such as chromium polynicotinate and chromium picolinate have been found to be the most potent and the easiest for the body to absorb. Romaine lettuce is an excellent source of chromium, while onions and tomatoes are also very good sources of this mineral. Other food sources of chromium include brewer's yeast, oysters, liver, whole grains, bran cereals and potatoes. Many people do not get enough chromium in their diets because of food processing methods that remove the naturally occurring chromium in commonly consumed foods. (For more advice on coping with a sweet tooth, see Chapter 5.)

Hopefully, after reading this chapter you will have some useful tools to help you zap unhealthy eating habits. Many things about depression are uncertain, but one thing isn't: a healthy diet can improve your health and well-being and increase the power of any medication you are taking. Remind yourself of that truth several times a day; write it down and stick a note on your mirror in the morning, or on your desk at work, or pin it on your fridge, or even write it on your biscuit tin. If the going gets tough, this will remind you that by taking charge of your diet and making positive food choices, you are doing all that you can to keep depression at bay.

10

Finding the motivation

The motivation to change your lifestyle has to come from within. It is like stopping smoking – no one else can make you do it, you have to *want* to do it. The trouble is that when you are feeling low and worthless, just getting out of bed in the morning seems impossible – so how on earth are you supposed to muster up the enthusiasm to change your eating habits?

Change your mind!

To find the motivation you need to make the depression diet a success, you first have to change your mindset. Below are some motivational mindset-changing exercises designed to help you do just that:

What might be

A good way to get started on any major life change is by using 'away from' motivation. Conjure up powerful images of how you will look and feel if things don't change in your life. Let these images impact you. You might want to use a 'Scrooge' exercise technique where what your life could become if you *don't* make changes is an incentive for change. Perhaps depression alienates you completely from your family and friends, or you lose your job because of it? Such techniques can be quite frightening, but sometimes you need a gentle reminder of what might happen if you don't take care of yourself.

What could be

This time, instead of dwelling on what will happen if you don't change your eating habits, put some energy into picturing how happy and healthy you could feel and look if you took care of yourself. Imagine yourself happy, energetic, in control of your life, and able to cope with your problems. Now link this vision with healthy eating and regular exercise. See yourself eating healthy food and enjoying it. See yourself having lots of energy to exercise. This isn't something you do just once. You need to do it over and over again on a daily basis until it becomes a habitual way of thinking. Spend some time daydreaming and make a mental 'film' of yourself looking healthy and living a healthy life. In your mind, watch that 'film' over and over again, whenever you need a boost.

Keep going

You can help yourself stay patient and positive with daily motivational statements, night and morning, such as: 'I'm looking and feeling good'; 'The quality of my life is improving every day'. This may sound unconvincing, but affirmations really can help. They won't stop you feeling depressed, but they can give you that extra boost of motivation or 'ommph' when the going gets tough.

Pat on the back

Congratulate yourself on a daily basis when you get something right: for example, making a healthy eating choice, walking to work, whatever it is. Get into the habit of patting yourself on the back. We all have a tendency to dwell on mistakes or bad feelings, so when you do something right, make sure you treat yourself to a walk in your favourite park, a funny film that makes you cry with laughter, a day out with your partner, a phone call to a treasured friend, and remember that feeling.

Hang in there!

Healthy eating and regular exercise can be a big help with your moods, and the sense of accomplishment can add a new dimension to your day – something you can be proud of and feel good about every day. Whatever you do, don't give up. Take things slowly, one step at a time, be gentle on yourself, and don't lose heart if you mess up (we all do!). Sometimes you just have to do what is right for yourself and wait for the good feelings to come later.

Depression is not just a chemical or nutritional imbalance. It can be a response to the need to address imbalance in our whole lives and is in many ways a transformative, healing process: the darkness before the brightness of a new dawn. Healthy eating is an empowering tool that can help you beat depression and give you the strength and energy you need to address imbalances in other areas of your life. It might help to think of the depression diet as a stepping stone to positive change and success in all areas of your life.

So now that you know food can influence your mood and increase your chances of happiness, eat well, savour the moment, and enjoy your daily dose of self-help on a plate.

The 10 Golden Rules for Mentally Healthy Eating

1 *Eat breakfast*: People who eat breakfast feel happier and mentally sharper than those who skip breakfast.
2 *Drink plenty of water*: Getting dehydrated can increase fatigue.
3 *Have protein-rich snacks*: This enhances the production of the neurotransmitters that improve mood, alertness, ability to cope with stress and mental functioning.
4 *Combine quality carbohydrates with protein and/or fat*: This will help to stabilize and sustain blood sugar levels – and consequently your mood.
5 *Get as much exercise and fresh air as you can*: This boosts your circulation and the production of the 'feel good' endorphins.
6 *Eat plenty of fruits, vegetables and whole grains*: These provide B vitamins and the natural antioxidants necessary for healthy brain function.
7 *Get your omega-3s*: About half of the brain is fat. Omega-3 fatty acids are required for transporting nutrients into the brain cells. They also help to regulate the chemicals that influence brain function.
8 *Keep healthy snacks to hand*: Almonds, bananas, cashews, dried fruit, blueberries, fig bars, hard-boiled eggs, hummus, instant oatmeal, low-fat cheese, oranges, peanut butter, pumpkin seeds, nuts, cereal, wholegrain crackers or pitta bread, low fat yogurt.
9 *Eat more, not less*: Don't leave more than three hours between meals or snacks. Going for long periods of time without food can trigger imbalances in the levels of neurotransmitters, and this can impact mood and thinking.
10 *Enjoy your food*: A delicious and healthy diet is one of life's many pleasures. Never forget you *deserve* to enjoy your food and your life.

Useful addresses and websites

UK

Allergy UK
3 White Oak Square
London Road
Swanley
Kent BR8 7AG
Tel.: 01322 619898
Website: www.allergyuk.org
Email: info@allergyuk.org

British Association for Counselling and Psychotherapy (BACP)
35–37 Albert Street
Rugby
Warwickshire CV21 2SG
Tel.: 0870 443 5252 (8.45 a.m. to 5 p.m.)
Website: www.bacp.co.uk
Email: bacp@bacp.co.uk

British Association for Nutritional Therapy (BANT)
27 Old Gloucester Street
London WC1N 3XX
Tel.: 08706 061284
Website: www.bant.org.uk
Email: theadministrator@bant.org.uk

British Nutrition Foundation
52–54 High Holborn
London WC1V 6RQ
Tel.: 020 7404 6504
Website: www.nutrition.org.uk
Email: postbox@nutrition.org.uk

Depression Alliance
212 Spitfire Studios
63–71 Collier Street

London N1 9BE
Tel.: 0845 123 23 20
Website: www.depressionalliance.org
Email: information@depressionalliance.org

Eating Disorders Association
103 Prince of Wales Road
Norwich
Norfolk NR1 1DW
Tel.: 0870 770 3256
Website: www.edauk.com
For anorexia, bulimia and other eating disorders.

Fellowship of Depressives Anonymous
Self-Help Nottingham
Ormiston House
32–36 Pelham Street
Nottingham NG1 2EG

Food and Mood Project
PO Box 2737
Lewes
East Sussex BN7 2GN
Website: www.foodandmood.org
Email: info@foodandmood.org

The Manic-Depressive Fellowship (MDF)
MDF The Bipolar Organisation
Castle Works
21 St George's Road
London SE1 6ES
Tel.: 08456 340 540 (UK only); 0044 20 7793 2600 (Rest of world)
Website: www.mdf.org.uk

Mental Health Foundation
London Office
9th Floor, Sea Containers House
20 Upper Ground
London SE1 9QB
Tel.: 020 7803 1100

Website: www.mentalhealth.org.uk
Email: mhf@mhf.org.uk

Scotland Office
Merchants House
30 George Square
Glasgow G2 1EG
Tel.: 0141 572 0125
Email: scotland@mhf.org.uk

MIND (National Association for Mental Health)
Granta House
15–19 Broadway
London E15 4BQ
Mind*info*Line: 0845 766 0163
Website: www.mind.org.uk
Email: contact@mind.org.uk

No Panic
93 Brands Farm Way
Telford
Shropshire TF3 2JQ
Helpline: Freephone 0808 808 0545 (10 a.m. to 10 p.m., 365 days a year)
Helpline from outside UK: 0044 1952 590545
Website: www.nopanic.org.uk
Email: ceo@nopanic.org.uk

Overeaters Anonymous
P.O. Box 19
Stretford
Manchester M32 9EB
Tel.: 07000 784985
Website: www.oagb.org.uk
Email: oagbnsb@hotmail.com

SAD (Seasonal Affective Disorder) Association
PO Box 989
Steyning
West Sussex BN44 3HR

Tel.: 01903 814942
Website: www.sada.org.uk

Samaritans
The Upper Mill
Kingston Road
Ewell
Surrey KT17 2AF
(In crisis write to: Chris, PO Box 90 90, Stirling FK8 2SA)
Tel.: 020 8394 8300 (admin)
Helpline: 08457 90 90 90 (24 hours, every day)
Website: www.samaritans.org
Email: jo@samaritans.org

Sustain Alliance (for better food and farming)
94 White Lion Street
London N1 9PF
Tel.: 020 7837 1228
Website: www.sustainweb.org
Email: sustain@sustainweb.org

Vegan Society
7 Battle Road
St Leonards-on-Sea
East Sussex TN3 7AA
Tel.: 01424 427393 (9.30 a.m. to 5 p.m., Monday to Friday)
Local Rate: 0845 4588244
Website: www.vegansociety.com

Vegetarian Society
Parkdale
Dunham Road
Altrincham
Cheshire WA14 4QG
Tel.: 0161 925 2000 (8.30 a.m. to 5 p.m., Monday to Friday)
Website: www.veg.soc.org
Email: info@vegsoc.org

USA

Depression Awareness, Recognition and Treatment (DART)
National Institute of Mental Health
5600 Fishers Lane, Room 14C03
Parklawn Building
Rockville, MD 20857
Tel.: (00 1) (800) 421-4211
Website: www.nimh.nih.gov/healthinformation/depressionmenu.cfm

Depression and Related Affective Disorders Association (DRADA)
8201 Greensboror Drive, Suite 300
McLean, VA 22102
Tel.: (703) 610-9026
Toll Free: 888-288-1104
Website: www.drada.org
Email: info@drada.org

The Food Allergy and Anaphylaxis Network
11781 Lee Jackson Hwy., Suite 160
Fairfax, VA 22033-3309
Tel.: (800) 929-4040
Website: www.foodallergy.org

National Alliance on Mental Illness (NAMI)
Colonial Place 3
2107 Wilson Blvd
Suite 300
Arlington, VA 22201-3042
Tel.: (703) 524 7600
Information Helpline: 1-800 950-NAMI (6264)
Website: www.nami.org

National Organization for Seasonal Affective Disorder (NOSAD)
PO Box 40190
Washington, DC 20016
Website: www.nosad.org

National Foundation for Depressive Illness (NAFDI)
PO Box 2257
New York, NY 10016
Tel.: (800) 248-4344
Website: www.depression.org

Australia

Mental Health Association NSW Inc
60–62 Victoria Road
Gladesville
NSW 2111
Tel.: 02 9816 5688 or 1800 674 200
Website: www.mentalhealth.asn.au
Email: info@mentalhealth.asn.

Useful websites

www.allallergy.net
A portal to hundreds of organizations, events, publications and products worldwide.

www.eatwell.gov.uk
A site run by the Food Standard Agency with advice on food safety, food labelling, and more.

www.faia.org.uk
A site provided by the Food Additives and Ingredients Association.

www.supportline.org.uk
SupportLine provides confidential emotional support, and details of other agencies, groups and counsellors in the UK.

Further reading

Cantopher, Tim, *Depressive Illness: The Curse of the Strong*. Sheldon Press, London, 2006.

Dryden, Windy and Opie, Sarah, *Overcoming Depression*. Sheldon Press, London, 2003.

Geary, Amanda, *The Food and Mood Handbook*. Thorson, London, 2001.

Horwood, Janet, *Comfort for Depression*. Sheldon Press, London, 2003.

Marshall, Fiona, and Cheevers, Peter, *Coping with SAD*. Sheldon Press, London, 2002.

Somer, Elizabeth, *Food and Mood: The Complete Guide to Eating Well and Feeling Your Best*. Henry Holt, New York, 1999.

Zuess, Jonathon, *The Wisdom of Depression: A Guide to Understanding and Curing Depression Using Natural Medicine*. Three Rivers, New York, 1998.

References

1 www.mentalhealth.org.uk/feedingminds
2 Alaimo, K. *et al.* (2000), 'Family food insufficiency, but not low family income, is positively associated with dysthymia and suicide symptoms in adolescents', *The Journal of Nutrition*, April, 132(4): 719–25.
3 Siefert, K. *et al.* (2001), 'Food insufficiency and the physical and mental health of low-income women', *Women and Health*, 32(1-2): 159–77.
4 Spillmann, M. K. *et al.* (2000), 'Tryptophan depletion in SSRI-recovered depressed outpatients', *Psychopharmacology*, 155(2): 123–7.
5 Crow, L. *et al.* (2006), 'Psychosocial and behavioral correlates of dieting among overweight and non-overweight adolescents', *Journal of Adolescent Health*, May; 38(5): 569–74.
6 Eby, G. *et al.* (2006), 'Rapid recovery from major depression using magnesium treatment', *Medical Hypotheses*, 14 March, 67(2): 362–70. Epub 2006, 20 March.
7 Banki, C. M. *et al.* (1985), 'Cerebrospinal fluid magnesium and calcium related to amine metabolites, diagnosis, and suicide attempts', *Biological Psychiatry*, 20(2): 163–71.
8 Rogers, P. J. (2000), 'A healthy body, a healthy mind: long-term impact of diet on mood and cognitive function', *The Proceedings of the Nutrition Society*, 60(1): 135–43.
9 Beard, J. L. *et al.* (2005), 'Maternal iron deficiency anemia affects postpartum emotions and cognition', *Journal of Nutrition*, February; 135(2): 267–72.
10 Markus, C. R. *et al.* (1998), 'Does carbohydrate-rich, protein-poor food prevent a deterioration of mood and cognitive performance of stress-prone subjects when subjected to a stressful task?', *Appetite*, 31(1): 49–65.
11 Chris, L. *et al.* (2001), 'Mood and carbohydrate cravings', *Appetite*, April; 36(2): 137–45.
12 Ohara, A. *et al.* (2005), 'Omega-3 fatty acids in mood disorders', *Seishin Shinkeigaku Zasshi*, 107(2): 118–26; Bruin, K. *et al.* (2000), 'Dieting, essential fatty acid intake, and depression',

REFERENCES

Nutrition Review, April; 58(4): 98–108.

13 Walton, R. *et al.* (1993), 'Adverse reactions to aspartame: double-blind challenge in patients from a vulnerable population', *Biological Psychiatry*, 1–15 July; 34(1-2): 13–27.

14 Bourre, J. *et al.* (2004), 'The role of nutritional factors on the structure and function of the brain: an update on dietary requirements', *Review of Neurology* (Paris), September; 160(8-9): 767–92.

15 Bodnar, L. *et al.* (2005), 'Nutrition and depression: implications for improving mental health among childbearing-aged women', *Biological Psychiatry*, 1 November; 58(9): 679–85. Epub 2005, 25 July.

16 Ras, N. *et al.* (2005), 'Insulin resistance in depressive disorders and Alzheimer's disease: revisiting the missing link hypothesis', *Neurobiological Aging*, December; 26 Suppl 1: 103–7. Epub 2005, 11 October.

17 Liap, I. *et al.* (2006), 'Interrelationship of hepatic function, thyroid activity and mood status in alcohol-dependent individuals', *In Vivo*, March–April; 20(2): 293–300.

18 The Feeding Minds Report published in January 2006 is free and is available to download from www.mentalhealth.org.uk/ feedingminds and www.sustainweb.org

19 Koukouvov, G. *et al.* (2004), 'Quality of life, psychological and physiological changes following exercise training in patients with chronic heart failure', *Journal of Rehabilitation Medicine*, January; 36(1): 36–41.

20 'Effect of vitamin and trace-element supplementation on cognitive function in elderly subjects', *Nutrition*, 2001, September; 17(9): 709–12.

21 Goldberg, I. K. (1980), 'L-tyrosine in depression', *Lancet*; 2: 364.

22 'Clinical studies on the phenylethylamine hypothesis of affective disorder: urine and blood phenylacetic acid and phenylalanine dietary supplements', *Journal of Clinical Psychiatry*, 1986; 47: 66–70.

23 'Inositol augmentation of lithium or valproate for bipolar depression', *Bipolar Disorder*, 2006, April; 8(2): 168–74.

24 'Nutrition and depression: implications for improving mental health among childbearing-aged women', *Biological Psychiatry*, 2005, 1 November; 58(9): 679–85. Epub 2005, 25 July.

REFERENCES

25 'Rapid recovery from major depression using magnesium treatment', *Medical Hypotheses*, 2006.

26 'Omega-3 polyunsaturated fatty acids and depression: a review of the evidence and a methodological critique', *Preventive Medicine*, 2006, January; 42(1): 4–13. Epub 2005, 7 December.

27 'S-adenosyl-L-methionine: effects on brain bioenergetic status and transverse relaxation time in healthy subjects', *Biological Psychiatry*, 2003; 54: 833–9.

28 'Role of selenium depletion in the effects of dialysis on mood and behavior', *Medical Hypotheses*, 2002, July; 59(1): 89–91.

29 'The role of nutritional factors on the structure and function of the brain: an update on dietary requirements', *Review of Neurology* (Paris), 2004, September; 160(8-9): 767–92.

30 'Zinc: the new antidepressant?', *Nutrition Review*, 2006, January; 64(1): 39–42.

31 'Superior efficacy of St John's wort extract WS(R) 5570 compared to placebo in patients with major depression: a randomized, double-blind, placebo-controlled, multi-center trial [ISRCTN77277298]', *BMC Medicine*, 2006, 23 June; 4(1): 14.

32 'Nutrition and depression', *Explore* (NY), 2005, November; 1(6): 474–6.

33 'Characteristics of depressive behavior induced by feeding thiamine-deficient diet in mice', *Life Science*, 2001, 27 July; 69(10): 1181–91.

34 'The role for vitamin B-6 as treatment for depression: a systematic review', *Family Practitioner*, 2005, October; 22(5): 532–7. Epub 2005, 17 June.

35 'Homocysteine and folate metabolism in depression', *Progress Neuropsychopharmacol Biological Psychiatry*, 2005, September; 29(7): 1103–12.

36 'Clinical relevance of low serum vitamin B12 concentrations in older people: the Banbury B12 study', *Age and Ageing*, 2006, July; 35(4): 416–22. Epub 2006, 18 May.

37 'The effects of ginkgo biloba extract (LI 1370) supplementation and discontinuation on activities of daily living and mood in free living older volunteers', *Phytotherapy Research*, 2004, July; 18(7): 531–7.

38 Grub, B. *et al.* (1999), 'St. John's Wort extract: efficacy for menopausal symptoms of psychological origin', *Advances in Therapy*, July–Aug; 16(4): 177–86.

39 Hallfrisch, J. *et al.* (1995), 'Diets containing soluble oat extracts improve glucose and insulin responses of moderately hypercholesterolemic men and women', *American Journal of Clinical Nutrition*, February; 61(2): 379–84.

Index